Club Fed

Living Inside a Women's Prison

Lynn R. Hartz, Ph.D.

PublishAmerica
Baltimore

© 2003 by Lynn R. Hartz, Ph.D.
All rights reserved. No part of this book may be reproduced in any form without written permission from the publishers, except by a reviewer who may quote brief passages in a review to be printed in a newspaper or magazine.

First printing

Names have been changed or altered to protect the identities of those involved.

ISBN: 1-59286-353-1
PUBLISHED BY PUBLISHAMERICA BOOK PUBLISHERS
www.publishamerica.com
Baltimore

Printed in the United States of America

Dedication

This book is dedicated to all women who are or have been in prison, but especially my roommate, “Diamond Kelly.” A better friend could never be found on the inside or the outside of a prison.

I also dedicate this book to Sylvia Kelly, my dear friend on the “outside.” She wrote to me faithfully, and is still a dear, true friend.

There is a very special woman who without her I would not have completed this book. She is Arline Chase, who was first my writing instructor and now my wonderful friend. She made certain that I told my story so that you, the reader, would know me and the lives of others which I have described for you.

From the bottom of my heart, I dedicate this book to Mitch.

I give my dearest thanks to all who helped with ideas and suggestions. I am proud to know each of you.

Prologue

It is extremely difficult to find information about women in prison. Some resources are available, but they are usually written from an academic viewpoint, which usually makes it less available to the public, and perhaps less readable.

I found myself a professional woman who had never had any prior legal problems, convicted and incarcerated for crimes I did not commit. Trying to understand how this could happen to me, and finding other women with similar problems, led me to develop this book.

Who are the women in prison, and why are they there? Most of them could be your next-door neighbors.

I was sent to a federal penitentiary without a trial. Spirit put me there, and Spirit got me through it. This is how it happened.

Chapter 1

Welcome to Club Fed

What AM I doing here? Who are these other women, and what did they do to be sent to prison?

For twenty years I had been a practicing psychotherapist. I had a Ph.D. behind my name. Honesty, truthfulness, and integrity were qualities that I valued in my life. So, how did I end up in prison? My anger was controlled, but I could feel it gurgling beneath the surface inside my body. *Darn it! I thought the government's legal system was designed to be fair*! I don't know why I thought that, but I was dead wrong. *At least I am not dead,* I thought, even though I felt dead inside my soul. *Will I be able to relate to any of these women*? The unknown loomed heavily before me.

The sentence was to serve twenty-one months in prison, because I had been found guilty of six counts of mail fraud and one count of obstruction of justice. (I had billed my patients' insurance for services rendered.) To this day, I still maintain my innocence on these charges. I never had an opportunity to tell the truth adequately. How can personnel in government service be so insensitive to people? It is more important for the prosecutor to win a case than to present the truth. Even as I reflect upon what happened to me, I feel outraged.

Because my life was devoted to helping people, I was totally baffled by the turn of events in my life. Not only was I furious with the government, I was angry at God. How could a kind, loving God, to whom I had devoted my life since I was young, allow something like this to happen to me? There was nothing about this that made any sense.

Not only did I not understand, I didn't *want* to understand. If God allowed this to happen, did He have no power? Was God punishing me for something that I did? The rules that the insurance company gave me were followed to the letter, so that was not the problem. It had to be something else in my life. Could I be a bad person, and not even be aware of it?

I was soon to realize something different about God.

The Spanish Girls

"Lynn, the Spanish girls are looking for you." As Gayle Rogers approached me in the cottage, I felt a little apprehensive. I knew Gayle, because she was the inmate whose job it was to coordinate orientation and interpretation. Gayle was one of the dark Spanish women from Puerto Rico. I was unaware that she was a Spanish woman, because her English was meticulous, and she didn't have a Spanish name. She was extremely well-educated, having two Masters' degrees, and she was multilingual. Gayle had taught political science in various Spanish-speaking institutions.

"I don't know any Spanish girls," I told her.

Looking directly into my eyes, she countered, "Well, they were looking for the woman that knows things, and you're the only new woman here that I know that *knows things*." Smiling as I listened, I *knew* that Gayle knew that I *knew things*. I had promised to do a spiritual reading for her, and had all intentions of doing that in the next couple of days. "And," she added, "they know you are here."

The only Spanish-speaking woman that I had met was Gayle.

"This is so confusing," I told her. "I can't imagine who they are, or how they know me."

"We're going up the hill to a meeting, so I'll introduce you to them while we're up there," she offered.

By this time, I was extremely curious. *Who* were the Spanish girls, and *why* did they want to meet me?

Alderson Federal Prison Camp for Women is located in Alderson,

West Virginia. It sits on the Greenbrier River, and it is actually located in Monroe, Summers, and Greenbrier counties.

Alderson is the oldest federal women's prison in the United States. It was conceived as a governmental need in 1925, and was built in 1927. The plan for the facility was developed from the college campus of Bucknell College, and the setting resembles a college campus. It is filled with trees, flowers, and tiny animals. Squirrels, chipmunks, groundhogs, and raccoons abound there. There are also birds: hawks, crows, blue jays, sparrows, starlings, and an occasional cardinal to brighten things. The buildings look like college dormitories.

There are no gates. The only fence is around the children's play yard in the visiting area. The gate has been missing since sometime in the early 1970's. Someone had taken it down, and no one knew what happened to it. It reminded me of that James Garner movie *Support Your Local Sheriff,* where the jail cells didn't have any bars on the door openings. He drew a line on the floor, dripped some red paint to look like blood, and told the prisoner, "Don't step over that line or I'll shoot ya'."

Arrival

There is a telephone where a gate used to be. As soon as they receive a call, a guard drives out and picks up the new "commit."

Upon first entering the prison, it is difficult to distinguish the staff from the prisoners. The staff doesn't wear uniforms, but the correctional officers (guards) do. The prisoners wear their own clothes, making the distinction between staff and inmates even more difficult.

There is one thing that I learned quickly: When you enter the prison, whether you are staff or inmate, you are supposed to leave your brain outside. There should be a sign that reads: "Check your brain at the gate! Everyone! Just enter and don't think! Do as you are told!" That is the basic attitude found in correctional institutions.

There are several ways of physically getting to prison. A person may self-surrender. In other words, you can drive yourself to the gate and come on in. That is how I arrived. My companion, Mitch Frazier, drove me down, and had to leave me at the gate. He said that was the most difficult thing that he ever had to do. The alternative is to be escorted by the U. S. Marshals. This means that the prisoner is brought in handcuffed and chained. The Marshals can bring the person either by automobile or by airlift. I was to learn that the flights are called Con Air. (There is a movie by the same name starring Nicholas Cage.)

Upon arrival, the first procedure is to process the prisoner. This reminded me of taking an inventory of a store. It is important to remember that prisoners are the property of the United States government, and *that is all.* Anything that a woman brings with her is inventoried, then she's fingerprinted, and pictures are taken for her files. One of the female officers strip-searches her, and escorts her to medical services for a quick medical check and medications, if needed. Then, she is given a room in a cottage where the new arrivals stay.

Cottages and Roommates

Rooms inside the cottages where the women live are about six feet wide by nine feet long. No closets exist, but the room is so small that it feels like one. The beds are bunks from an ancient war that was long forgotten. Springs on the beds sag, and the person on the top bunk practically lies on top of the person in the bottom bunk.

The first two weeks are considered orientation time. This time is slow for the new inmates, because there are meetings to learn about the various departments in the prison. Each person is given a physical, TB test, other blood tests, psychological tests, and a tour of the campus.

The upper level of the campus sits on a small hill. There are four cottages, the recreation hall, the library, and the chapel. There is also a softball field, and the inmates have several softball teams.

The lower level has the visitors' facility, the education building, the administration building, and food service. There are seven cottages on the lower level. Behind everything else, next to the railroad tracks and next to the Greenbrier River, are the administrative offices for facility maintenance.

Who's in Charge Here?

The first impression, because the assumption is logical, is that the staff is in charge here. Wrong! Wrong! Wrong!

Staff is here to count. Now remember that because sometimes they can't even count correctly. But that is staff's main purpose, and no one has to be able to count above one hundred. One person, however, must be able to add a few numbers for a total.

The inmates run the prison. They cook, clean, rake leaves, drive other inmates out of the prison to appointments, work as tutors, library aides, hospital aides, secretaries, electricians, plumbers, painters, construction workers, powerhouse workers, and carpenters. The inmates do their best to let staff believe that they are in charge and in control, but, the truth is, even the staff knows that the inmates run the prison.

"Ya' Got a G.E.D?"

Education is supposed to be of prime importance in a federal prison. During orientation we were taken to the department that is called education.

A man who is supposed to evaluate the educational needs of each inmate asked me, "Ya' got a G.E.D.?"

"No," I replied. "I have a Ph.D."

The next thing he told me was, "If you don't have a G.E.D., you have to go to school."

In total amazement, I gasped. "I have a high school education and four college degrees. Why would I be expected to go to school to get a G.E.D.?"

"Oh," he reacted blankly.

In one quick moment, I discerned the educational level of the people who were supposed to be in charge of the prison.

An inmate without a G.E.D. or a high school education is only paid four cents an hour for the work she does. Some of the women need the few cents that they earn just to exist while they are in prison.

The prison has about 125 Spanish-speaking women, and they may have a high-school education. However, they are often expected to take the G.E.D. and pass the test, even though the G.E.D. is not offered to them in their own native language.

There are some other types of apprenticeship programs available in plumbing, electrical, powerhouse, and construction. Secretarial and administrative assistant courses are available, as well as a dental assistant program. A woman may take college courses through correspondence, but she has to pay for the courses herself.

Get a Job

"Get a job," is the first thing I was told. Getting a job actually meant finding a place for the inmate to be during the daytime. Some of the jobs, such as landscape and ground maintenance, were actual work. Other jobs consisted of sitting most of the day and doing very little of anything else.

"If you don't get a job, you'll have to work in food service, " I was told by a staff member during orientation. I couldn't understand what the problem was with working in food service, but it apparently had a very bad reputation for a lack of camaraderie between staff and inmates.

Finding a job seemed to be more a matter of whom you knew rather than what kind of skill you had, and what you could do to best serve the institution. If you remember, the rule is to leave your brain at the gate, so, if what you would like to do makes any sense, it will definitely be denied. What the staff wanted seemed to be sheer, brute labor, not intelligence.

The women worked as library aides, clerks, secretaries, receptionists, maintenance workers, landscape workers, plumbers, masons, electricians, boiler room laborers, cooks, waitresses, dishwasher operators, warehouse laborers, teacher aides, drivers, and chapel aides.

I applied for everything that was not physically exerting. I was assigned to the kitchen and sorted silverware every day. Remember, I said if it made any sense, your request would be denied. Having a Ph.D. and sorting silverware every day did not make any sense. One of the women who sorted silverware with me had a degree as a doctor of veterinary medicine.

I noticed that the chores women least liked were the ones they usually had to do. As a child I hated washing dishes. Going to college and being educated was my way of ensuring that I would be able to buy a dishwasher and *never* have to wash dishes again! Silverware was always the part of washing dishes that I hated most.

So, I thought like Pollyanna, the little girl who was called the "Glad Girl" in the Disney movie. I was glad that we had silverware, and that we didn't have to eat with our fingers or plastic utensils. I was glad we had a machine to wash the dishes. I was glad that most of the food service building was air-conditioned. I was glad that I only had to sort silver twice a day. I was glad we had food, and plenty to eat. I became really good at being glad.

New Lingo

Soon after I arrived in prison, I had to learn a new lingo. There are abbreviations for everything and words to describe situations.

The first new word I learned was "shot." A staff member writes an "incident report" for something that requires disciplinary action against an inmate. That is a "shot."

"They shot somebody? Oh dear! What did she do?" Patty Johnson was an attractive, slightly overweight white female in her mid-thirties. She had pretty brown, wavy hair, a beautiful smile, and was so innocent when she arrived at the prison. Whatever she did to cause her to be incarcerated could not have been a major offense, because she had never been in any trouble or had any experience with jails or prisons. Patty did not adjust well to the prison. She had health problems, also, so they sent her to Carswell, Texas, to a medical facility. Patty's crime was that she had not fired an employee who was embezzling money from where she worked. She was found more responsible for the crime than the employee, because she didn't fire him or report him to her superiors. Her sentence was longer than his.

Another frequently used term was "cop out." In most prison and legal settings, this term means to "plead guilty" or "beg for mercy." That term is valid, but in the federal women's prison system, it means an inmate's request to a staff member. "Cop outs" were used for a multitude of purposes, including a job inquiry, a service needed, such as medical, a request for an appointment, or a law student.

There were initial abbreviations used for a variety of things. CDR meant Center Dining Room where the food services were staffed. R & D was short for receiving and delivery. That represented persons, packages, and mail. It is important to understand that in prison, people are property. The government actually owns your body, and you are a commodity, something which must be accounted for several times a day.

Admissions and Orientation are referred to as A&O. There was a separate building where the new inmates stayed until they were moved into a permanent cottage. Some people refer to this building and processing as the "bus stop," meaning that the new prisoners would stay there only until they would be moved to their new cottage and room. New inmates are called "commits." Again, the prisoners are commodities, not "people."

Everyone talked about the BOP until it just became common language. The BOP is the Bureau of Prisons, an agency of the Department of Justice. The women of Alderson were their "guests."

"Count" refers to the time when inmates are counted, which is several times a night and once a day.

Every day a list of names of inmates would be posted on a paper called the "call out." That list would show cottage changes, work assignment changes, educational changes, and any appointments, such as dental or health service.

Some staff was in charge of collecting fines and restitution for crimes and that was referred to as "FRP"—Federal Restitution Payment.

Inmates refer to food service as the "slop house." Ms. Jackson, a food service cook foreman, said that when she first started working at Alderson more than twenty years ago, they were told they had to provide "three hots and a cot."

"Pill line" referred to picking up prescription medicines or taking medicine that is not allowed to be taken without staff supervision.

The "po-leece," meaning "police," is the term that some inmates use to refer to the correctional staff.

A "detainer" is possible pending court action that would prevent release of an inmate.

When an inmate is ready to leave prison, she has to take release papers to a various department to be signed. The lingo for this process is "merry-go-round."

Count Time!

The most important thing that the staff had to do was count. Most people learn to count to one hundred during kindergarten. I did. You probably did, too. However, the only important thing that the staff had to do was count, but they never, ever got it right. It was frequent that a "recount" was needed. The number of inmates had to match a number sent from the BOP. There were two women who escaped, at different times, and that created a problem. Those were legitimate wrong counts, but miscounts occurred too often otherwise.

***

It wasn't long before Gayle introduced me to Martina Estevan. She was from Columbia, South America, and spoke with a deep Spanish accent. She was shapely with long auburn hair and deep set, snappy brown eyes.

Enthusiastically, Martina called to me, "I'm so glad you finally got here."

"What do you mean, you're glad I finally got here?" I wondered why anyone would ever be glad that someone finally arrived in a prison.

"We knew you were coming." Martina smiled broadly, revealing beautiful teeth and an exhilarating personal warmth.

"Oh, you mean you saw the TV coverage about me?" I thought worse things than I care to mention about all of that publicity from the trial.

"No, no, no. Don't you understand? We were told the same way you are told things that you would be here. We didn't know your name; we just knew you were coming. We prayed you here," Martina said softly as she touched my arm.

"You prayed me here!" I was flabbergasted. "Why?"

"Oh, we didn't know it would be you," Martina continued. "We have been praying for God to send us someone to teach us spirituality and healing. We were told that you would be here before we leave Alderson," she explained.

"You mean to tell me that you all prayed that someone would come to the prison who would understand your spiritual needs, teach you spiritual truths, guide you in how to work with the various aspects of spirituality, and you didn't even know for whom you were praying?" I was astounded.

"That's right," Martina confirmed. "We're sorry you're here, but we need you. Will you teach us?"

My response was an unequivocal, "Yes." Suddenly, I understood some things that I hadn't been able to comprehend. There *was* a divine purpose to the craziness that I was experiencing. It would be a little while before I really understood the reason why I was there.

Chapter 2

What Did You Do to Get Here?

It seemed the first question anyone asked was, "What did you do to get here?"

Women are sent to prison on a wide variety of charges. Statistics show that approximately one-third of all cases are drug charges, and/or conspiracy related to drugs.

In a women's prison a large proportion of crimes are related to money, such as bank fraud, forgery, mail fraud, using someone else's money fraudulently, or insurance fraud. In order for most of these to be federal crimes, the crime has to relate in some way to the federal government, such as a check being processed through the mail or a bank. My case was federal because the checks from the insurance company had been mailed through the U.S. postal service.

Some women say that they don't know what they did to get in prison. One of the officers told me that those people are almost always in prison for conspiracy, or obstruction of justice. There are too many of these to even enumerate.

Tax evasion is another crime for which women are imprisoned. A woman's husband may have had her sign the tax form as the spouse, which makes her equally as guilty as he, if there is any criminal intent. She may be unaware of any criminal activity, but she is responsible for her signature.

Money laundering is another crime for which women are imprisoned. These women may or may not have actually hidden money or assets, but the implication can be attached and a conviction won, even without proof.

Many of the women suffer from mental illness or mental retardation, but that doesn't change the crime or the sentence. There were several women who fell under the new "Battered Spouse Syndrome." However, that was not used for their defense. Most of the women who commit "money" crimes suffer from depression or manic depression and have never been treated for their illnesses.

Other crimes, such as air piracy, gambling (running a gambling business), probation violations, and welfare fraud make up the rest of the prisoners' offenses.

Probation violations are interesting. A violation can be anything from a "dirty" urine (drugs) to a marriage that wasn't authorized.

One woman, who became angry when her ex-husband wouldn't answer the telephone, shouted into the answering machine, "If you don't answer the phone, I'm going to kill you!" She was sent back to prison for making a threatening telephone call.

Another woman, who married without the consent of her probation officer, was sent back to prison because she had a change in her financial status and didn't notify the government. This constitutes the commission of an additional crime in the eyes of the government.

A few husbands have been known to turn their wives in for probation violations for the use of drugs or alcohol. They think they are "helping" their spouses, and the women are returned to prison. However, most of them don't have enough time to receive any help in the drug program.

One of the first people I met, "Lady Di," asked me that question, "What did you do to get here?"

Diane was a large, red-headed woman who worked in food services. She had been in prison for almost four years when I arrived, and had gained an enormous amount of weight while incarcerated. She was still a pretty woman, with beautiful brown eyes, a pretty smile, and dimples. Her appearance was immaculate, her makeup perfection, and her clothing as clean and coordinated as was possible.

Diane earned the nickname "Lady Di" from Ms. Jackson, one of the food service supervisors. Ms. Jackson also called her "Pebbles" because she was originally blonde when she arrived, and she pulled her hair up in a topknot like the littlest Flintstone. She even had a very large purse with "Lady Di" written on the side.

Diane was liked by some and disliked by others. She continued to work in food services, which was the main work assignment most women wanted to avoid. Few women could tolerate the food service staff, because they treated the inmates rudely. Diane seemed to be able to take everything in stride.

"So, what did you do to get here? You were a doctor, and you can't work anymore?" she prodded. There was no getting around an answer.

"Okay," I agreed. "Here's my story."

A Life-Changing Accident

"Watch out!" I heard the voice of Jonathan, my angel, as clearly as I could see the car driving head-on into me.

With a knee-jerk reflex, I hit the brake, but I knew that it wasn't going to help.

Metal met metal, crashing and crushing upon collision. Glass shattered as the side of my head hit the window. As my leg smashed into the transmission console, I could hear the bone snap. The impact was invasive. I could feel the separation in the bone, and I knew it was broken, probably in two places.

"Oh, God. At least I'm not dead," I said thankfully to God and whatever angels were listening.

In only seconds, I heard police sirens and saw ambulance lights. The fire station was only a few feet away, and the ambulance was sitting there.

I rolled down the window and handed the policeman my driver's license.

"How badly are you hurt?" he asked.

"My leg is broken in at least two places," I calmly told him. "I bumped my head pretty hard, too."

"We're going to get you out of the car and to the hospital."

"Please call my mother. Ask her to please go take care of my daughter." Grace, my youngest daughter, was eleven years old and waiting for me to come home from work. She knew that I would be late, because I was going to pick up a friend and take him to the Red Cross to donate blood for a surgery I was to have the following week. "Then would you please call this number?" I handed him Ray Landers' phone number. "He will contact my boyfriend for me."

The policeman handed the information to another officer, and he started to take care of that detail.

The Emergency Medical Technicians (EMTs) started work, attempting to get me out of the car. Before they tried to move me, they took my blood pressure.

"Darn it," I said to the man taking my blood pressure. "I have my favorite clothes on today." He couldn't get my sweater high enough to get the blood pressure cuff on my arm.

"We're going to have to cut your sweater off," he told me. That was my favorite sweater! If I could keep from ruining it, I would. I tried to take it off myself, but it wouldn't come off. I could not move enough inside the smashed car to manipulate my arms and pull it over my head.

Better my sweater than my life, I thought. I always tried to be practical when things happened that I could not control.

The EMTs put a cervical collar around my neck so that my head wouldn't move. Then they pulled me out of the car and onto a stretcher. My leg hurt so badly I thought I would faint.

Once I was inside the ambulance, they had to take my boots off. These were my favorite boots. They were bright red, and I had decorated them with beads and silver conches.

"I think we're going to have to cut your boots off, too," the EMT told me.

"Try wiggling them off first. These are my favorite boots, and I'd like to save them, if possible."

He tried, but it hurt too much. "If you have to cut them, then cut down the seam and I'll try to have them sewn back together." With the skill of a surgeon he made a nice, smooth cut. I knew he was being cautious. He showed it to me when he took my leg out. The cut was right on the seam; I sew, and could not have done better.

My leg was so swollen that the boot would not have come off without being cut.

I was in the hospital for nine days. The snow was more than three feet deep the day the doctor did the surgery on my leg. Mitch, my companion for the past two years, tried to pick up my mother so that she could be with me during the surgery. However, the snow was too deep for her to get out. My dear brother, Ray, was there when I awakened. Amazingly, he ventured out in that horrible storm to be with me while I had surgery.

An odd thing happened while I was in the hospital. The newspaper took a picture of the snow, and it was on the front page of the newspaper. The picture had my house in it, and Mitch's truck was in the driveway.

"Isn't it nice that they put our house on the front page of the newspaper? I'm sure they did that just so I'd know everything was okay at home," I teased my daughters when they came to visit.

I had met Mitch Frazier two years prior, at an Indian cultural meeting. We started seeing each other, and the relationship became stable and secure. Mitch and I resembled each other in coloring. We both had brown hair and hazel eyes. He was six feet tall, and worked as a welder for the power company. He was a very private individual and lived outside of town on a small farm. His most remarkable feature was that he had no right hand or arm below the bend of the elbow. His personal outlook on life was that he liked the "old ways." In other words, he would have been content if society had never left the turn of the century.

Nine days later I left the hospital with a forty-five pound cast on my leg and a walker to help me mobilize. The cast was so heavy that I could barely move myself around on the walker. The streets and sidewalks were still icy, and I had to be very careful getting into my house. Going upstairs was another problem. That cast stayed on my leg for five weeks, then it was changed and a walking cast was put on. That cast was on for another five months.

All that time I was unable to work. My business deteriorated quickly.

The week I had the cast removed, another crisis arose.

***

"Mitch, some FBI men just stopped by the house. They are investigating me for something, but I can't figure out what they want," I told him when I awakened him.

"What's going on? I thought all that stuff was over," he said sleepily.

"So did I. They came to the house, and one of them said that he was a former client of mine, but I didn't recognize him. I told them that I had a lawyer, and they should have contacted her, but they said this was something different. I can't imagine what they think that I've done now," I mused while changing my clothes. This lawyer was a female public defender who had been handling my defense of the previous investigation of my company. I didn't much care for her or trust her, but she was all I had at that time. I certainly didn't have any money to hire a lawyer.

"What are you doing?" Mitch asked as he filled his pipe.

"I'm changing my clothes and am going to have someone take me down to my office," I answered. A sleeping shirt was all that I had on when those men came to my door.

"What are you going to do down there?"

"Ask Edna and Darlene if they've heard from these men, and look for the files of these people," I planned as I talked to him.

"Are you sure you can walk well enough?" He was concerned because the cast was off my leg for only a few days.

"I think so. I'll take my cane," I responded, trying to get my shoes to fit over my swollen feet.

"Be careful, and if you need me, call," he instructed. He was very protective of me since I was hurt.

"I will." I kissed him goodbye. My body was tense, and I was anxious as my friend drove me to my office.

When I got there, I made a few notes in the charts and told the women that they could give them to Will, our lawyer, to handle for us.

That was the beginning of another phase of an investigation into my business. The federal government had investigated my business five years previously, but had never charged me with anything criminal. Now they had started it again. I wondered what they thought I had done this time.

Bankruptcy

Meanwhile, I still was unable to work, and I knew that the inevitable had to be done. As much as I resisted the idea, my business had to be bankrupted. I couldn't handle the business anymore, and I couldn't even think about working, so I filed for social security disability. I had no idea how I would manage without an income or a way to earn a living.

"Will, I can't deal with the stress of working, and I'll never be able to pay all of the bills," I told Will on the telephone. "Who can I get to help with a bankruptcy?"

Will Sullivan was my former husband's best friend from high school. "Billy and Willy" was how they were known. Bill was over six feet tall, and Will was a few inches under six feet. When Will was young, he looked like a blond John Travolta in *Grease*. I had known him since I was fifteen years old.

Will was the valedictorian of his high school class, as well as the editor of the newspaper, drum major for the band, and almost all the other honors that could have been bestowed on anyone at the high school level. Will was given a scholarship to Harvard University, where he completed his undergraduate work. He married, had three children, and graduated from law school at West Virginia University. His wife died when she was in her early thirties.

Will had problems with alcohol, which he would not recognize. He functioned well for an alcoholic, but his astute reputation was fading. He had been appointed a special prosecutor, and he had prosecuted election fraud in West Virginia in the mid 1970's.

When the legal problems began, I called Will for help. A sideline to the legal problems was that he and I began seeing each other when I first called him, which was several years before I started seeing Mitch. It wasn't long, however, until Will started seeing my nineteen-year-old daughter. I was devastated and shocked. It was months before I could handle the situation with my daughter and him.

Will always said, "Where there's a Will, there's a way," and, despite his lack of romantic dependability, I trusted his legal expertise.

He had recently gone into partnership with another lawyer from Huntington, Donald Cook, then, just as suddenly, left the partnership.

"Why don't you let Don handle it for you?" Will suggested.

"Do you think he can right now, since he's going through his own problems?" I asked. The FBI was investigating Don for something related to a client's money.

"He is an excellent tax and bankruptcy lawyer," Will informed me. "He could use the business. I'm sure."

I thought about contacting a local lawyer first, because I didn't feel like driving to Huntington to see someone. It was a fifty-mile drive, and I was unable to drive anywhere. I had not driven anywhere since the automobile accident.

"What are you going to do without your business?" Will asked.

"I'm not able to work anymore, Will. The stress is unbearable. I can't think straight, and I can't remember things. I filed for social security disability the first of July. Now, can you see me working with patients, doing psychotherapy, when I can't even remember them or what their problems are?" I did my best to explain what was happening so that he would understand.

"You'll never get disability approved," Will retorted. "You have to have something permanently wrong."

"Well, I guess I won't die, even if they don't approve it," I snapped. His negativity irritated me. I knew I was not functioning well, and he should have known, too, since he'd been handling my accident case for the past few months. "If I have to get a lawyer for the Social

Security, do you want to handle it?" I knew that would put him in a spot.

"No, I don't think so," he laughed. "I want cases where I can make some money, and I don't think you will win this one."

"Okay. Thanks for the help. I'll call Don." We hung up with our usual personal clash and irritation.

A few weeks later after the bankruptcy was filed, I met with the bankruptcy judge.

"Here are all the accounts that I haven't been able to collect for the business." I handed him a stack of papers. "Some of them are rather old, and I don't know what to do about them. I thought Mr. Cook should have had all this information for you," I told him. I wondered what Don Cook had done for the money I had paid him.

"We'll see what we can do with these," Judge Smith told me. "Now, there's a problem about your house. It might have to be sold to cover the liabilities," he continued.

My heart sank. That house was all I had. "It wouldn't sell right now because it needs so many repairs, and there are so many liens on it that there wouldn't be any way to cover anything else," I explained to him. He had the information about the indebtedness, but didn't realize that my house was involved.

"Oh, I didn't realize that," he told me. "We'll just leave it as it is. What is your mortgage?" he asked.

"About $350 a month," I replied. "I couldn't live anywhere else any less expensively," I added.

"We'll just leave the house alone, then," he answered.

I felt immense relief. I didn't have a job or much money. I didn't have a business anymore. But I did have a house.

It didn't take long for the bankruptcy to be complete. I was notified in October that it was final. All I had was a house that needed a lot of attention and a very old car.

Indicted on the Television News

"Be careful!" I told Dr. Edward. "I can't stand to have my eyes touched. It makes me nauseated and dizzy. Just don't do anything without telling me exactly what you're doing." I dreaded anything done to my eyes, especially if it meant any kind of examination.

I had no idea what had gotten in my eye, but it hurt so much that I couldn't sleep, and whatever was in it needed to come out. That's when I went to the doctor in the emergency care facility.

"I promise to be careful," Dr. Edward told me. "I understand not wanting to do something that makes you anxious." He lifted my eyelid and looked inside with a magnifying glass and light. "There doesn't seem to be anything in it," he mused. "Now, I want to turn your eyelid up and look at the inside. Do you think you can do it?"

I felt sick just thinking about him turning my eyelid inside out, but I bravely said, "Yes. Just be gentle and careful." While I shuddered, he took my eye lid and rolled it up so he could see under it.

"I can't see anything in it," he concluded. "There might be a scratch on it where something was, and that might be causing the pain. Let's put some medicine in it, patch it, and check it again in a couple of days."

Valiantly, I drove home with a patch over my left eye. It was difficult judging distance, because there is no depth perception with just one eye. I was extremely careful.

As soon as I arrived home, I telephoned Mitch. "The doctor patched my eye, and he couldn't see anything foreign in it. It still hurts, but he prescribed some medicine, and I stopped at the pharmacy to pick it up. The rest of the day, I think I'll just rest."

"Don't you know what you did to it?" Mitch asked. "What do you think happened?"

"I don't know. If I did, I would tell you, but I just don't know. I'm tired of things happening to me. Every time I turn around it's something else. I would give up, but I don't know how," I lamented, almost whining. *Why doesn't this bad stuff go away and leave me alone, or at least pick on someone else*?

I sighed to myself. Tears were coming, but I knew I didn't dare cry, because it would cause my eyes to water, and that would make my eye hurt even more.

Finishing my telephone call with Mitch, I called my mother. My mother knew how sensitive I was about my eyes.

"Do you have to put drops in your eyes?" Mom asked. That was something another person had to practically hold me down to do.

"Yes, but I don't have to put them in until tomorrow. I think Mitch will help me," I told her. "Mom, I just don't know what else can happen to me. Do you think I did something bad to create all these things going wrong?" I felt paranoid, or very close to it.

"Honey, you do seem to have more than your share of things happening. Maybe this is it for a while," she comforted.

"I'll talk to you later, Mom. Thanks for listening. By the way, don't forget that today is Beethoven's birthday," I reminded her. It was usually mentioned in the *Peanuts* comic strip on December 16, but I hadn't seen it this year.

I guess I can listen to the news, even if I can't see the TV very well, I thought as the 11:00 news came on. I had slept through the early evening news, and it was important for me to know what was going on in the world, even if I wasn't able to be out and around very much.

"The U.S. Prosecuting Attorney announced that the grand jury has indicted a local counselor on mail fraud charges. Dr. Lynn Hartz…." The TV news anchor droned on and on. I thought I was hallucinating.

June, a close friend of mine, called and asked, "Lynn, did you hear the evening news?"

My voice sounded dead as I cried, "I can't believe it! I'm in shock."

"You didn't know about this?"

"Heavens no, I didn't know! It seems to me that I should have been informed before it was plastered all over the news, but I wasn't. I did not give up my right to testify in front of the grand jury, either," I told her. She knew that the investigation had been off and on for years. I had actually written on an earlier notification that I did not wave my right to appear before the grand jury. "Let me get off the phone and call Mitch at work."

"Mitch," I said, as calmly as I could, "I've been watching the late night news, and I've been indicted by the federal government on charges of mail fraud."

With his temper flaring, Mitch shouted. "What? I thought all of that was over by now! What else did they report?"

I explained that all they said was that I was indicted on four charges of mail fraud, and I had no idea what it was about.

"Remember today when I said I wonder what else could happen? Well, now we know."

The next call I made was to Will.

Lawyer Dismissed by Judge

I did not even try to contact the lawyer who had been appointed by the court when the investigation started. I knew that she would not handle this case well and, after all, she was paid by the government, the same as the prosecutor. I didn't trust her any more than I trusted the people in the U.S. Attorney's office.

Will tried negotiating with the U.S. Attorney's office, but he didn't get anywhere. I was arraigned, then released on a personal recognizance bond.

Meanwhile, the U.S. Attorney handling my case left the office. This was now the fourth prosecuting attorney on my case. It appeared that there was a problem in that office, or that it was a springboard to something else.

All that I was offered was to plead guilty to some charge, and I'd get six months' probation.

"Will, I am not guilty. I can't do that."

Less than three weeks later, something else occurred.

"Will, they've done it again," I told him on the telephone.

"What?"

"More indictments…and on the television again." I spoke dazedly.

"How many more?" he pressed.

"They said three superseding indictments," I managed to say. "One of them is supposed to be obstruction of justice."

"They told me that they were not going to pursue anything related to that. It seems to me that I should have been notified, since I *am* your legal counsel. Those b------s don't play fair," he exploded.

"Does that mean we have to go back in front of the magistrate and all that stuff?"

"I think so, but I'll find out for sure. "

Back to court, I thought. *I hate that place. If I never have to go there ever again in my life it will be too soon.*

***

"Why are they doing this?" I asked Will, when Harold Hunter, the prosecutor, told the judge that Will should be dismissed from the case because he could be a witness.

With frustration, Will mused, "I don't know. They do not play fair, and they will use anything that they can in order to win a case." We had to go back to court again, this time to see if he could stay as my lawyer.

***

" So…do you think this is just another ploy? All they want is for me to plead guilty, and I am *not* guilty. I am sick of this! I don't want that public defender to handle my case, because she was never there when I wanted to see her." She had written me a note that was not very nice, too, and I considered it a threat. That's when I knew that I had to have Will handle this case. I didn't know how I would pay him, but then Mitch decided that he would pay Will for me.

"Will they hold a hearing on this?"

"I'm sure they will."

The hearing was held the day I had a doctor's appointment, so I didn't hear the proceedings, while Will had to defend himself as my lawyer.

Will told the court that he advised the people who were in my office to write down their recollections of various patients before they testified before the grand jury. The prosecutors said these notes were improperly submitted as patient records.

The article in the newspaper the next day was headlined "Lawyers may be witnesses, so he's told to step aside."

I now had seven indictments, no lawyer, and no money. What was I supposed to do next?

***

Three weeks later the judge appointed a new lawyer, Mr. Carroll Emerson. I met with him, and he told me that another lawyer in their firm was interested in working on my case with him. So, I had two lawyers, Carroll and Sam Jensen. Now, two lawyers sound positive, but Carroll had never won a federal case, and Sam had never worked on a criminal case. Both of them were accustomed to only practicing civil and corporate law.

In Prison, but Not a Prisoner?

"Judicial discretion! What in heaven's name is that?" I practically shouted at my new lawyer. "Whatever it is, it isn't right!" I protested as loudly as I dared. "What could give a judge the right to send me to prison without a trial? I haven't been convicted of anything!"

"Well, it means that he has the right to do whatever he thinks is necessary in this case," my new lawyer told me. "But we can appeal his decision and try to get it overturned," he told me. My doctor had written the judge a letter telling him about the accident, and that I suffered from a head injury which kept me from remembering things correctly.

This combination of information was just what the prosecutor needed in order to legally harass me more than he had already. The headlines in the article in *The Charleston Gazette* read, "Counselor May Be Suffering from Depression." I thought, *Yeah, right. With this kind of thing going on, who wouldn't be depressed?* Reading the article *did* make me depressed.

My new lawyer talked a good game, but, as I was to find out later, he did not play the game very well. He was a tall, slender man who ran on a daily basis. He told me many things about his life. Both of his parents had been doctors, but he left home at an early age and made his own way in the world. He worked his way through college, and then worked as a carpenter. One of the people he had worked with dared him to attend to law school, so he applied, took the tests, and was accepted. He accepted court-appointed cases, especially drug cases, because, he told me, "Drug cases are not treated fairly." Before the trial I found out that Carroll had never won a federal court case.

There had been four different prosecutors on my case. The first was a woman, Janet Patton, who was appointed a county judge. She was later forced to resign when the F.B.I. investigated her for "bugging" her estranged husband's law office and taping his telephone calls. The next lawyer went to work for an insurance company, and the lawyer that followed him resigned, entered private practice, and died.

This U.S. attorney's name was Harold Hunter. It recently occurred to me that men with the first or last name "Hunter" seem bent on professions in law enforcement, such as policemen, detectives or prosecuting attorneys. Defense lawyers are not named Hunter, or at least none that I have noticed. His demeanor was that of a hunter. His height and body structure reminded me of a sleek, dark panther, ready to pounce on an innocent kill.

Sam Jensen, the lawyer who volunteered to work with Carroll on my case, was interested in problems with insurance, medical billing, and psychological situations. My case met all of those criteria. Sam, a heavyset man with glasses and light brown hair, was a family-oriented man with five small children, and his demeanor was kind and sympathetic. His work had brought him into contact with my brother, Andy Richardson, who was West Virginia's Commissioner of Employer Programs, which included Worker's Compensation and Employment Security.

The situation suddenly made me laugh. *I had been in the psychiatric-psychological field as a professional therapist for twenty years, and now this judge wanted to send me to a prison hospital to find out if I was competent! Could this predicament be any more absurd?*

I thought about this situation for a while, and then decided that I wanted the lawyers to appeal this court order. The appeal would take time, so the lawyers asked for a "stay," which meant that I would not have to go to the prison until a hearing and decision by the Fourth Circuit Court of Appeals was heard.

I was teaching at a community college, and had asked for a change of a reporting date in order to complete my end of semester responsibilities, and that was granted. Grace, my youngest daughter, was still in school, and I would have to make arrangements for her to be cared for while I was gone.

By the time the hearing was held on the stay, it was the day that I was to report to Lexington Federal Women's Medical Prison in Lexington, Kentucky.

The hearing was held in front of a Fourth Circuit Appeals Judge, and the appeal was denied. I was to realize later that all judges uphold each other's decisions almost without exception.

I went home and told Mitch that we needed to go to Lexington. My anxiety level was high, and he was angry. All I could think was, *I have to go to prison and I haven't even been convicted of a crime.* My anger level went higher and higher. I wondered if I would explode in rage.

The drive to Lexington was two and a half hours long, but it seemed to last an eternity. Judge Harper said that it was "only about an hour and a half to Lexington," when he had made the decision that I was to go to prison for a competency evaluation. I wondered about this man's knowledge of local geography, because I knew that it took two and a half hours to get to Lexington.

"Judicial discretion," Mitch spouted. "Judicial b–l s--t!" I had never seen him as angry as he was when we arrived at the prison. There was chain link fence and concertina wire surrounding the prison. I was terrified and angry. It was difficult to know which was the stronger emotion.

All I could think was, *Dear God, what did I do to deserve this?*

"Goodbye, Mitch." I kissed him. "Don't worry. I can stand anything for a month." I had no idea what was coming next.

My heart sank as his red and white Ford pickup truck drove away. He told me later, "I never felt so entirely and completely helpless in my life."

Chapter 3

Locked in a Prison Mental Ward for a Month

Arrival

When I arrived at the prison in Lexington, Kentucky on Monday, May 16, 1994, I was locked in a cage. *Why are they locking me in a cage?* I wondered. *What are they going to do to me? Am I safe?* I was sure I wasn't safe.

Processing meant that I had to remove my clothes and be strip-searched. Never had I experienced anything as humiliating in my life. The guard told me I had to bend over, squat, and cough. Then I had to lift my breasts. I sobbed quietly, from fright and embarrassment. The pain I felt in my body actually made my skin hurt. I was so anxious that I shook all over. Then a female guard took all my clothes away from me.

Before I went to this prison, I called and asked what I could take. I took paperback books because they told me I could. But they took those from me as well. They told me I could take my sleepwear, and I sleep in long T-shirts, but they took those away, too. The clothes I had worn—my green silk suit jacket and print skirt—were put in an envelope and mailed to my home. I knew they were going to be really wrinkled when I returned. My sandals, bras, and panties were all that I was allowed to keep. Then I was given blue pants that were much too long, a blue shirt, and a dark blue, long T-shirt to sleep in.

A guard told me that I would be issued clothing from my unit. I was told that I couldn't alter the clothing, not even to hem the pants so that they would fit. Later, I realized that this scenario was a psychological ploy to humiliate people and gain control over them.

A guard escorted me to the mental health unit, and a nurse interviewed me and took me to a cell on the second floor, with a toilet and sink in it. The door was steel, with bars on the windows, and a slot to put a food tray through. *She is locking me in a cell and I haven't even been convicted of a crime.* I wondered, *How long it will it be before I can see people again?* She took all of my medicine away from me and said that the doctor would have to evaluate me before I could have any. She told me that I wasn't a prisoner, so they wouldn't lock my door at night, and the next day they would give me a room. Later, I learned that they don't lock anyone's door unless there has been a flagrant rule violation.

I never felt so abused and frightened in my life. All the time I was being processed and all night long, I cried. When I talked with the nurse, she wrote in my file that I was angry and hostile. I told her, "I have no right being here. I am not supposed to be a prisoner, but here I am, locked up without anything to read or do." I was awake all night.

The following day, I met Doctor George Roberts, a psychiatrist. He appeared nice enough, as far as his personal demeanor, but I had to repeat what I said to him three times. I wondered why, if he were a good psychiatrist, he was working in a prison hospital. He was going to give me back my medicine, but they didn't have Ritalin or lithium in tablet form. One medication, Ritalin, is the same medication that is given to hyperactive children, and I took it and lithium for my head injury. The liquid lithium caused me to vomit, so I refused to take any more of it. They did a complete blood work in the morning before breakfast, as well as a urinalysis.

When I finally had breakfast, it was cold eggs and warm milk. It was inedible.

Clothes

I was moved to my own room on the first floor, but I still didn't have any clothes to wear, or a comb. Although I asked repeatedly, I couldn't figure out what the problem was. If the goal of this craziness was to wear me down, I was beginning to wear. I cried all day. The guards said it was the counselor's responsibility to issue clothing and personal items, but he was on vacation. Why a male counselor would be on a woman's mental health ward was beyond me. The women told me that they didn't even talk to him. Later, I was to find out that a prison counselor doesn't do counseling. All they do is take care of various business or prison related discipline.

I felt so deserted and alone. My body and hair were dirty, and I couldn't shower because I had no towels or soap. This was obviously one of the most inefficiently run places I had ever seen. Inefficiency drives me nuts, especially bureaucratic inefficiency.

Two days later I still had no clothes, comb, or towels. I started crying uncontrollably as soon as I awakened, and I couldn't stop. *If those people worked for me, they'd have soon found themselves unemployed,* I thought.

Mrs. Ware

Mrs. Jean Ware, a correctional officer, was very kind. She was a short, plump, dark-skinned woman with a great amount of hair. She wore blouses and skirts as her uniform, and she looked professionally perfect. When I started crying, she calmed me down. Then she called Mr. Shrewsberry, a counselor in another unit, and asked him if he would get me some clothes. He had another staff person, Ms. Barnett, who was a recreation specialist, bring me some clothes, and Mrs. Ware gave me a comb and shampoo. She was good to everyone. She should have been doing counseling because she was empathetic and could see right through people.

The following day I had nothing to do, so I did a spiritual reading for Mrs. Ware. I am able to sit with a person and know things about them. I found a very sensitive thing that had happened to her, and she said that she had never told anyone about it. She told me about things in the prison. Then she went on vacation for nine days, and I thought I couldn't stand it until she came back.

Ms. Ware had a four-year college degree in sociology and took a job working for the prison because it paid well, and she didn't have to travel anymore. Before she started working for the prison, she had worked for a Multi-Cap program in the nutrition area, and was not paid well and traveled all the time. I told her that I turned down that same position in West Virginia years ago, for the same reasons. It was obvious to me that she was a blessing to the women prisoners and definitely to those locked into the mental health unit.

When Mrs. Ware was gone for nine days, I didn't think she'd ever come back! When she returned, her hair was fixed with braid extenders, and she was in really good spirits. She won $176 playing the lottery with the numbers I told her to play. Ware was a character! I would like to have her for a friend.

Blood Pressure Problem

In the afternoon I was given a complete physical by Dr. Chandler. He was an understanding man. He took my blood pressure, and it was 210/160, which is stroke level. He had the nurse get Precordia immediately, and put it under my tongue. "You are about to explode," he told me. I admitted how angry I was because I knew this work could be done on an outpatient basis, and he agreed. My blood pressure had never been a problem, but it has continued to this day. He did a pelvic exam and a breast exam, then ordered a mammography. On Friday I had a chest x-ray, which took about five minutes. My leg was supposed to have been x-rayed, too, but they didn't have that on the order.

It was over a week before I got my leg x-rayed. The results of that should have been back about a week later.

My blood pressure continued to elevate every time I thought about the injustice that was being done, not just to me, but to several others I met in the mental health unit.

Ordinary Events

Later in the afternoon, I met a Comanche Indian woman. She was supposed to teach some crafts. I really enjoyed meeting her. She was the only one who had boosted my spirits after I had arrived. The next day, however, I was told that she left to go to another prison closer to her home and I didn't get to spend any time with her.

I found a quiet room with chairs and a TV. I thought that might help my stress.

The receipt for my commissary account was finally given to me. My money hadn't been credited to my account, so I didn't get to go to the commissary.

Dr. George, the Psychologist

On Friday Dr. George, the psychologist who was in charge of my "study"—not to be confused with Dr. George Roberts, the psychiatrist—had me sign release forms to get my records from Charleston Area Medical Center, and Dr. Joseph Whelan, my own psychiatrist. That did not take very long. What was it about the prison and legal system that everything took longer than necessary?

Dr. George also tried to get it worked out for Mitch and Ray, my brother, to visit, but the people he needed to see to get the order faxed over and back were not there.

Dr. George was not a personable, friendly man. He didn't seem to care what happened to people. I think he believed that everyone who was evaluated was guilty of a crime.

He took his time doing the work that was supposed to be done on me. It was several weeks before I did the MMPI (a major personality test). I never waited so long to do the same or similar kind of work in my business. It was usually the first thing that I did. He had the total prison population to handle psychologically, but it didn't appear to me that he was in any hurry to do anything. *A typical bureaucrat,* I thought. *As long as they have a paycheck coming in, time is not a matter of great concern.*

Food

Dinner that Friday evening consisted of lasagna, salad, cookies and toasted buns. Most of the food was really good for institutional food. It was better than anything that CAMC hospital served when I was injured.

The weekends were different. In the early mornings coffee and sweet rolls were served, and then brunch was served about 10:30. No one told me that this was how it was done, and for a while, I was confused. We were allowed to sleep late on the weekends, which was why that was done.

Breakfast was never very good. They made biscuits that tasted like hard, unbaked dough that had been in the refrigerator for a month.

Jenny Price

One of the prisoners, Jenny, had an emotional eyesight problem. She, basically, chose "not to see." She was a woman in her mid-fifties who had some kind of legal trouble related to nursing homes and Medicare billing. Jenny was sentenced to ten months in prison, but, because of the problem with her eyesight, she was sent to a medical prison instead of one closer to her home in California.

Jenny walked around holding on to the furniture and walls. I spent hours talking with her about the conflicting emotions and how those feelings related to her imprisonment. She was a short woman, about five feet tall, and had totally white hair, although she was only approximately fifty-five years old. A psychiatric nurse, she knew these things, but was emotionally unable to reconcile her feelings. It was obvious that the prison medical personnel had done nothing to help her, either through counseling or any other means. Jenny regained enough of her sight that she was able to be moved to another unit.

If my leg was hurting or swelling, she would massage it and work on it until it would feel better.

"I'm so happy you're here because there aren't many professional women in the mental health unit of the prison," Jenny confided. Her remark pleased me, and made me think that maybe there was a purpose for the things I was experiencing. Whatever that purpose was, however, wasn't legal.

Evelyn

Evelyn, a new "study case," was admitted the following week. "Study case" is what the women were called who were ordered by the court to be evaluated by the prison. Her name was Evelyn Taylor, and she had a stroke, which caused memory problems. Evelyn was shaking and crying early in morning while she was on the telephone, and I told her when visiting hours were. Then I told her to look me up as soon as she got off the telephone. I knew how she felt, because a week ago I had felt the same way.

When she found me, which wasn't difficult, because I was sitting at a table writing, she started telling me her story.

"I've been accused of conspiracy to deliver marijuana, but I didn't do it. The state dropped the charges because there wasn't enough evidence to prosecute me, so the federal government picked up on it. I cannot remember anything. I can't remember even things I read." She was about the same age as I, but unable to function very well.

First, I talked with her and calmed her down, then prayed with her. She said, "I am a Christian. I wouldn't do any of the things these people have accused me of, and I really don't understand it."

I told her I also was accused falsely, and that several people on the professional staff told me that these evaluations always helped the cases. However, it appears that with as much medical work and psychiatric work that she had experienced, her evaluation could also have been performed in outpatient setting.

Evelyn became my roommate, and I had to help her with her paperwork for the commissary. She knew that the commissary was a way for the prison to make money, even though she was unable to process the forms.

Clementine

It was two o'clock in the morning and Clementine, who had been in the mental health unit for a long, long time, was sitting outside on the deck. She was singing "The Star-Spangled Banner" as loudly as possible.

"Why are you singing, Clementine?" the tiny, fit, blonde inmate named Kathy asked.

Clementine, who was dark-skinned, probably six feet tall, over three hundred pounds, and definitely schizophrenic, answered, "I'm singing because I'm so happy."

Clementine loved me. She told me she did, and told me that I was a god.

"Clementine, I'm not God," I told her. Don't ever try reasoning with a schizophrenic. I'd tried before in my private practice, but I thought I'd try again.

"Yes, you are," she insisted. "I can see God right in your eyes." She looked at me with her own eyes wide.

Clementine was in prison for robbing a bank. I never did know her last name.

Bad Dreams

Guards checked the inmates twice a night. Some of them used a flashlight, practically shining it in my face. This had caused an undue amount of sleep disturbance.

My nightmares came back. I suffered from nightmares off and on most of my adult life. One night, I dreamed my mother slapped me in the face. Now, in real life, my mother has never hit me. In my interpretation, my country has always been like a mother to me—a nurturer, a protector, and a source for help in times of need. But now I found out just the opposite. If that doesn't constitute a "slap in the face," I don't know what does!

Another dream was that my mother kissed Hitler. Dream interpretation was always one of my professional strengths. My analysis was that it significantly represented what I felt about this country. It's as though this country had prostituted itself, and all the people here were like sheep, as they were in Nazi Germany. In a telephone conversation with Mitch, he said that he thought my mother believed that Lexington was just a hospital. I wondered if she understood that I was a prisoner for a crime for which I hadn't even had a trial?

I didn't sleep well most of the time because of the bad dreams, but I don't remember the content of them. Evelyn, the woman who shared my room, said I mumbled and cried out almost every night. When I finally would awaken, I was exhausted and extremely anxious. I awakened about 4:00 in the morning, and then had trouble going back to sleep. When 5:00 check came, I would still be awake.

The worst dream that I had was that I was raped by the prosecutor, Harold Hunter, and the counselor, Mr. Payne, while two nurses held me down and the judge (Claude Harper) and my two lawyers just stood by and watched. Upon awakening, I felt ill. I felt raped and vulnerable.

Brenda

One day I spent almost an hour talking to Brenda Ross, another "study," about rational thinking. Brenda was a very immature thirty-year-old with long, unkempt hair. She had a gun charge for buying a gun with false identification.

"I've been to counseling and would answer their questions, but nothing more," she told me. "You're easy to talk to," she continued. That was the first of many talks that we had.

There was also a Positive Mental Attitude group, and I suggested that she and I go to the group. The man conducting the group read out of a book. Very few participated in the group discussion. I could have taught that course so much better.

I wished I had a watch. I would have been able to keep track of the time I spent with the inmates doing what staff should be doing, but I wasn't going to pay $18.95 for a watch. My watch was taken from me when I came in. The commissary was a moneymaking racket if ever I saw one.

I made a collect call to my brother, Ray. There was no other way to call, and Ray was a kind, sympathetic person. He told me that Mom and Andy, my other brother, who was also a lawyer, were coming over to visit me. They arrived at 10:40 a.m., but I wasn't notified until 11:15 a.m., and then didn't get to see them until 1:30 p.m. because two people on other units were missing when the staff counted everyone.

"Lynn, I think this is another one of Harold Hunter's tactics, and that his case is so weak he is scared," Andy told me.

I told them about the nightmares coming back, and how I woke up terrified, crying, and unable to go back to sleep.

We did have a nice time together, playing cards, eating junk food, and talking. I still didn't know if Mom understood how bad this was, even though a guard stood outside the door of the stall in the restroom while she was in there. She might still believe that this was a real hospital.

We had been promised that a movie, *Geronimo*, would be shown that evening, but they canceled. I was very disappointed. *Indian givers*, I chuckled inwardly. As I thought about any kind of rational reason for not showing the film, I could not get Geronimo out of my mind. He fought against the federal government, and the soldiers followed him and his forty people across the Mexican border to bring them back to the United States. All Geronimo attempted was to keep forty people clothed and fed.

On Monday, May 23, 1994, I had been locked up for a week, and they still had done nothing in the way of testing or anything else. Dr. George brought me a copy of an order from Judge Harper ordering me to stay another fifteen days. He had a smile on his face when he handed me the order. I believed that this man had a tendency to sadism. That meant I could not leave before June 29. I cried until I felt sick, and I finally went upstairs and got the medicine to stop the anxiety.

I started writing poetry which I titled: *Not a Prisoner*. It seemed that I needed to be furious enough to start writing about it. Anger was my major modality at that time. With a different focus, I analyzed some of the good things about being in prison. Here's my list:

What's Good About Being in Prison?

1. You don't have to cook.
2. You don't have to go to the grocery store.
3. You don't have to work.
4. You don't have to answer the telephone.
5. You don't receive telemarketing calls.
6. You don't have to dress up and look nice.
7. You don't have to buy your own clothes.
8. You don't have to iron.
9. You don't have to wash dishes.
10. You can read as much as you want.

Much later, a friend of mine told me that it sounded like a vacation to her.

My blood pressure was still elevated. It was 168/101 and then later 148/94. I knew that anger was the reason.

A Redneck Counselor

I asked the counselor, Mr. Jack Payne, who was on vacation the previous week, six times in two days to make a private telephone call to my lawyer. He was the biggest redneck I had seen around the prison. Lexington. Kentucky is not in the heart of "Redneck Land." Lexington has much more of a "city" atmosphere. He chewed tobacco and spit in front of people. Talking to him was like talking to an answering machine without a message on it. He didn't pay attention to anything that was said to him. I gave up and called from the phone that is monitored.

One day the so-called counselor, Mr. Payne, came in and shut my door.

"Ms. Hartz, are you married?" Payne snarled.

"No," I answered. "Why?"

"A Mitch Frazier has called over here, trying to find out about visiting," he sneered as he chewed his disgusting tobacco.

"Mitch is my long-time companion," I said more nicely than I felt. I didn't think Payne needed any other explanation. He did approve the visit.

Another time he had been off for a few days, and when he came back, he was in a really bad mood. It didn't take long to figure out that he was a major problem in the mental health unit and probably with the prison staff.

A Real Psychologist

I finally met someone whom I believed understood my predicament and plight. His name was Carl Wright, a contract psychologist who was supposed to do psychological testing on me. We talked for over an hour, and neither of us seemed to want to stop. Dr. Wright told me that he would be back the following day to do some of the testing. I told him about the appeal process, and he asked when I thought I would be out of there. "A week from Friday," I told him. He said he would try to be finished by then, so that I wouldn't have to have the testing done again. He and I got along well together.

When I was talking to Dr. Wright, I told him, "I have provided more time in professional services than I had received."

"I promise you'll receive plenty of services this week," he smiled.

"I really don't want to do anything for the government," I told him, and he asked me to do what I could because the women needed help so badly. He said that most of the women in the total population were there because of something their husbands or boyfriends did that involved the women. Truly, what he was saying was, "Bloom where you are planted." I called Carroll immediately and told him about it. Carroll said that the brief to go to appellate court would be in by the end of the week. A decision would not be made by the end of the week.

Spirituality

I asked God when I would be out of this situation, and I was mentally instructed to read Jeremiah, which I did. Reading his experiences gave me strength and wisdom.

There was so much that I wanted to share with Mitch, but he was discouraging, and I couldn't talk or listen to negativity, and keep my faith. I would rather have had hope right then, and be disappointed later, than feel discouraged at that moment.

I did some hands on healing on one of the women. She decided that was why I was there—because I didn't push pills, and did provide healing. Her headaches went away and so did the pain from some other physical ailments. Several people were watching, including one of the staff nurses named Bobbie. She asked me if I would do a spiritual reading with her sometime. Unsure of what to say, I told her, "Maybe. I have to be in the right mindset to do that." I did not feel trustworthiness in this woman, but I didn't know why.

On Sunday, June 5, 1994, the church people came. I had not met them before, although they had been there. They had a short worship service, and then asked the women to share how God was working in their lives.

One man looked at me and said he could see the light of Jesus around me. He asked me to share what had been happening with me. I told them about being in prison, not being a prisoner, and how shaky my faith was at times. Patiently, I told them that I felt like Job, who had all the things happen to him, but he didn't lose his trust in God. Then I told them how Mitch's faith was lacking, and how angry he was. Expressing my disillusionment with our government, I compared myself with Jeremiah, who sat by the road and cried for his people.

I told them that I believed that God had a purpose in all of this, and that I had to do what He told me, because I didn't want to go to Ninevah in the belly of a whale like Jonah.

One of them compared my situation to that of Jesus. It was the chaplain who made that analogy. He said that Jesus didn't want to do what he was sent here to do, and he asked that "this cup pass from him."

But he did it anyway.

Several of the people said that I was their inspiration that day. They asked if I knew what I was supposed to do with this experience, and I told them, "Judicial and prison reform." Then I told them that I didn't want to do that, but since this has happened to me, I knew it could happen to anyone. All of them wished me well. One woman, Barbara, said that she would ask her angels to watch over me. They were inspiring people.

How to Survive

My items from the commissary finally arrived, and I had enough "brown pop" to last the week. I drink much too much cola, and the commissary only carried Coke. I much prefer RC.

Although I had not planned to buy any make up, I did. If I were to feel like a real human being, I needed to think that I looked decent. Next, I assigned myself a job. Every day I would get up, get dressed, put on my makeup, sit at my little bedside table, and write.

This plan worked, and I was able to write. My roommate, Evelyn, and I traded bedside tables so that I could have the one with the pullout writing tray on it.

Evelyn was the woman I mentioned earlier who had several strokes and had a memory loss. I became agitated at not having anything to read. People kept the TV turned on to things that were uninteresting or often violent. The TV was supposed to be off during specific hours, in order to "encourage" the women to participate in activities. There were absolutely no activities that I wanted participate in, even if I were able.

Recreation Director

The so-called "Recreation Director," Ms. Brown, reminded me of a high school gym teacher. She had an attitude and air of superiority around the prisoners because she was "staff." This attitude served only to make her look inferior in the eyes of others.

She promised to take me to the prison library to get some books, but she never did.

Counseling Inmates

I did the most incredible "house-tree person" on myself. The "Goodenough House-Tree-Person" is a psychological tool that is used to evaluate the cognitive and emotional processes of an individual. The person draws a picture of a house, a tree, and a person. It is evaluated by a process that looks for the emotional factors in the picture. I was excited about showing it to Dr. Wright. This tool showed my emotions, my cognitive processing, and my head injury! I had just been playing with it, because I didn't have anything to do. After I did mine, some of the other women wanted me to do theirs. I had them draw the pictures, and then I evaluated them.

Dr. Wright did some testing. It took about one and a half hours. He said he'd be back the following day to try to complete this work.

One of the nurses was rude to me about my medicine. I had to take the klonapin to calm down the anxiety. I felt out of control.

Talking to Mitch made my anxiety worsen, because he expected me to stay in the prison until June 29. I called Andy, and talked with him. He said he was going to talk to Carroll the following day.

Books

The books that were taken from me when I first arrived still had not returned, and Mitch had mailed them the day he brought me to the prison. When my books finally came, they were the ones Hope, my daughter, sent, not the ones Mitch sent. Darlene, my former secretary, also sent me her own Bible and two books. Tears flowed down my face when I saw her own Bible.

If that isn't one of the greatest gifts of love I have ever experienced, I thought.

It was almost four weeks before I received the books that Hope had mailed the first week I was there. She sent them priority mail. These were the same books that the prison sent back, unopened, the first week I was here.

I read all day, every day until I ran out of my own books, then someone would send me some more.

I found a book about Thomas Jefferson that was extremely interesting. Some of the problems he had with the Constitution and the power of the courts are the same problems that exist today. The cheques and balances do not work with the judicial system in this country. There are none. The judicial system makes law, instead of interpreting it. That is exactly what happened during Jefferson's times. He was a brilliant man—way ahead of his time in thought. It was an interesting book to read.

Memories

Thursday, May 26, 1994, was the anniversary of my husband, Bill's, death. I'd been in the prison for ten days. I'm sure he would not have been too happy to know that I was in prison, even if I wasn't supposed to be a prisoner. It was raining, just like it did the day I flew into Huntington with Nell, my oldest daughter, to bury him. I couldn't get to the cemetery the previous year because of my leg. Now I couldn't get to the cemetery because I was in a prison.

Handcuffs and Chains

They were supposed to take me to the University of Kentucky for a CAT scan on Friday, May 27. I wanted to get that done. After Friday, though, I was not sure if I could (not would) survive this situation. What a day!

I was supposed to get the CAT scan, so I was not to have anything except clear liquids to eat or drink. My breakfast was apple juice, Sprite and Jell-O. I didn't get any lunch. They took me downstairs, strip-searched me, then told me I'd have to have handcuffs and chains to be escorted out of the prison. I was *not* a prisoner!

As we walked down to where they put the chains on, I said, "I don't understand how someone who is not a prisoner can be treated like a prisoner. I don't want to do this. I will go, but not in chains and handcuffs." The more I thought about it, the more embittered I became. A guard told me that I could refuse, so I did.

I was trembling and shaking all over. I tried to call Carroll, but couldn't get him. Payne, the "counselor," started talking to me, "Now, Ms. Hartz, you know me…."

I said, "No, I really don't know you." Why he even started talking to me, I didn't know.

I went upstairs to the nurses' station and wanted to get my medicine. Two nurses jumped on me verbally.

"You have to sign a refusal form!" one of them shouted at me.

"What did you expect? You're a prisoner, and you have to be handcuffed and chained!" the second one screamed.

"How do you expect to have this evaluation done if you don't cooperate?" the first one bellowed.

I tried to keep my composure. I told them that I was not a prisoner, had not been convicted of anything, and should not be treated like a criminal.

"You have to sign a waiver of not having the medical work done. That's the rule!" the second of them barked at me again.

"I am not signing a waiver that said that, because that is not what happened. I refuse to be taken out of here in chains and handcuffs." A simple, quiet explanation would be better than venting the anger I felt.

One of them went to Mr. Payne, and he came to my room and put me in a locked cell for an hour.

One of those smart-aleck nurses came to the window and said, "Ms. Hartz, are you all right? Do you need anything?"

I said, "No."

A little while later she came to the locked cell and said that Dr. Chandler wanted to see me. He had the paper for the waiver, and he did it exactly the way I had told the nurses. I was still shaking so hard that my signature didn't even look like my writing.

I immediately tried to call Carroll and couldn't get him, so I called Sam. Talking to him calmed me down enough to stop crying. However, I was still kept trembling all over, and the medication didn't seem to help.

After I got off the phone with Sam, the nurse came down and asked if she could sit next to me. I told her, "No." It was a ploy to try to talk to me. There were plenty of other chairs around. It was my understanding that she was the person responsible for not telling me what to expect about going to the university hospital.

As long as either of those two so-called nurses were around, I wasn't taking my medicine. Just looking at them made me start shaking. Staying away from them became my medicine.

A few days later, I had to get a new card for the commissary, and, while I was there, I saw one of the files where I was to be taken out of the prison for the CAT scan. There was a comment on the form that said: "Ms. Hartz is very discontent with her situation and can cause a disturbance." I don't know who wrote that, but it was signed by the unit manager on Wednesday, June 1, 1994.

At that time I decided that I would eat with the others, but that was all. I decided to stay in my own room as much as possible. I would read and write and just not have any contact with anyone. Dr. George spent over an hour with me after the incident. Again, I repeated that I was willing to have the tests done, but I was unwilling to be chained and handcuffed.

"If the prison gets a court order to take me in chains and handcuffs, then I will go, but not voluntarily," I told him. "This work could have been done as an outpatient, and the court ordered me here to have the work done as an inpatient. It just doesn't make any sense for the prison to have to take me as an outpatient to do part of the work," I explained my logic to him. He affirmed that, then told me that he could only do what the court ordered. He did a complete case history, up to the time of my baby's death. Time was getting late, so we stopped. He was supposed to return the following Monday, even though it was a holiday, because he said he was behind on his work. The other psychologist, Carl Wright, was to finish the testing the following day.

Then I remembered something important. Even if they didn't get an EEG and CAT done, what difference would it make? We had already decided to leave our options open to having the evaluation done again. So what if the prison says that I'm not cooperative? That should have shown those evaluators that I would not be treated unfairly, and that I would stand up for what I believe.

I found strength in the song, "You've Got to Stand for Something, or You'll Fall for Anything." I'd changed other things in this world on a smaller scale, of course, but maybe that was training for changing some bigger, more important things in this world.

When I went upstairs to get my medicine that evening, Brandy, the nurse who had me locked up, tried to start a conversation with me about my visit, how long it lasted, and did I have a nice time. I didn't want anything to do with any of them.

They were supposed to do an EEG a few days later, but, again, that meant handcuffs and chains, so I refused to go. I was given the waiver to sign, and had to write out that I was not refusing the EEG, just the handcuffs and chains.

This was during the time that Mrs. Ware was gone, and I knew I'd be glad when she returned.

Sandy Lee

When I went to supper, I started to sit with Sandy, one of the women who was living on the same wing of the prison as I. She said, "If you're going to sit here and complain, don't sit here." Moving, I sat with Clementine, the psychotic who said I was a god. Throughout dinner I cried because Sandy hurt my feelings. We were friendly, and I didn't know what I did to offend her.

Sandy had a six-month sentence for something to do with a civil rights violation. She was from one of the states in the deep South. I didn't know why they had her in the mental health unit. I thought that she wouldn't be there if she were emotionally well-balanced. As I thought about it, maybe I wouldn't be either!

The following day, I did very little of anything except sleep and read. I was starting to read the third book, which was one that Darlene sent me.

Dr. Wright did some more testing on me. He said I did very well, neurologically.

Nursing Staff

When I went upstairs to take my medicine Bobbie, the rude nurse, made me open my mouth to see if I had swallowed my medicine.

"Maybe you don't know it, but I don't have to take my medicine at all," I told her. And that was true. It was my option because there was no court order or doctor's order for me to take any medicine. She was one of the nurses who had me locked up when I refused to leave of the prison in handcuffs and chains.

Later in the evening she came down to talk to me. She said that she did that with every third patient, but I'd never seen her or anyone else do it, except to Clementine. She also told me that Dr. Elrichman was the doctor who ordered me to be locked up. He didn't even see me. She said I was so upset that they were afraid I'd harm myself or someone else. When Pence came to take me to the locked cell, I was sitting in my room eating an apple. I was alone and was calming myself down. All they did was intensify my emotions, which were already raw.

There was a male nurse (John Cossin) who was abusive and abrasive to me because I was not having blood tests done.

He said, "It was ordered for your study. Are you saying you refuse? You flatly refuse?"

"Yes. I am not having them do any more damage to my arm," I answered, as amicably as possible. He treated me badly, spoke harshly to most people, and had no warmth in his personality. If you're not there to get your medicine precisely on the dot of the hour, he would come looking for you and berate you verbally.

He was one of these people who worked in the prison that wouldn't work for me for one day. Once they got a job with the government they know they can't be fired, so attitude doesn't mean anything.

Dr. Roberts talked with me for about twenty minutes one day. I told him why I wasn't getting the blood tests done, and he said that was all right because the lithium was not enough to ever become toxic. (I already knew that.)

Thoughts on Women Political Prisoners

I thought a lot about Margaret Sanger and Susan B. Anthony, women who went to prison for standing up for what they believed.

Margaret Sanger spent time in prison for teaching women about birth control. Susan B. Anthony was incarcerated for voting when it wasn't legal for women to vote. I most certainly hoped that I didn't have to endure their hardships, or length of time in prison, but I did hope that whatever happened, I would have an impact on women.

Tanya and the Haircut

Prison was worse than a zoo. One woman started cutting hair. She was apparently a new woman in the mental health ward. I never did know her name. She was absolutely the slowest person I had ever seen cut hair.

"I'm slow because I'm on medicine," she kept saying. She'd have been slow on anything. She took three hours to cut three heads of hair, and one of those was a trim.

Then Tanya Lawyton, a woman who had been in the mental health ward for a long time and had escaped from the prison once, decided that she wanted a "skin head" cut. The woman cutting hair didn't know how to do one. She started cutting, and had her hair all jagged with lines in it. One side was cut, and nothing on the other side was cut.

Then, suddenly, the woman cutting hair put down her tools and walked off crying, saying, "I don't know how to do it, and I'm tired!" That left Tanya sitting there with half of a haircut. Someone handed Tanya a very small mirror and asked if she wanted lines on her head. Tanya looked, then looked again, and very calmly said, "No."

Next another woman, Jackie, whose hair was cut very short and blocked, and who never wore makeup and had well-developed muscles, said that what Tanya wanted was a crewcut. She took the barber clippers and clipped all of Tanya's hair off.

The whole time this was happening, Ms. Ware was saying, "You can't leave Tanya like that. Look at this lobby! You can't leave this lobby like this!"

Then Mr. Payne came in and said, "Tanya, if I'd known you

wanted your hair cut like that, I could have done it for you. I know how to cut hair." Tanya was very happy with her hair cut.

Mr. Payne went into Ms. Ware's office and shut the door. I knew he was laughing. So was Ms. Ware. Ms. Ware was close to hysterical. Payne couldn't contain himself. He called and had a lieutenant come and take a picture of Tanya. She didn't seem to mind. It was Bureau of Prison rules to take a current photograph of a person if they altered their appearance.

Meanwhile, other women sat around in total amazement watching all of the goings-on.

Ms. Sampson

That same afternoon Ms. Ware answered the telephone. It was a friend of hers who worked outside the mental health unit. The officer, Ms. Sampson, was the same lady who was supposed to take me to get the CAT scan done.

She was telling Ms. Ware about me. "That nice lady that was talking to you before you went on vacation, she just went off, started crying and shaking and saying, 'I'm not a prisoner! I don't know why I need to be handcuffed and chained!' I ain't never seen nobody shake like that in my life! I don't know how you work over there with those people." Then, as Ms. Ware started telling me about it, we both laughed until we cried. I told her to invite Ms. Sampson back down and let her see that I was normal. We laughed again.

Caroline

Meanwhile, there was one woman who was becoming psychotic as we watched. She did strange things with food— packed it up and carried it to her room. She talked to herself or the floor and said nasty, smart-aleck remarks to people.

I said, "Ms. Ware, don't the doctors know what's going on with her? Don't they know she's acting psychotic?"

Ms. Ware said, "They haven't diagnosed her as psychotic yet."

I said, "Well, what the heck are they waiting on?" Then she and I started laughing again.

Kathy

Later in the evening Kathy needed some help. Kathy had been in prison for almost seven years on a drug related charge. She was a pretty, blonde-haired, blue-eyed woman, and had kept her weight and body beautiful. She expected to be released toward the end of the month and was truly looking forward to getting out.

Kathy wanted to have less light in her room, so she decided to disconnect three pairs of florescent tubes. In order to reach them, she had to fold a mattress on a bed, put a chair on top of that, then climb on the chair.

There were two of us holding the chair, myself and Brenda Ross. We laughed because it was getting close to time for the ten o'clock count, and Kathy couldn't be standing on a chair unhooking the lights when they came to count. We got two sets finished, put the mattress back on the bed, and the chair back on the floor.

They came through, counted, and left. We went back in Kathy's room and started on the other set of lights. This time we moved the mattress off one bed, put it on the other bed, then put the chair on top of everything. Kathy climbed on the chair, took the cover off the lights, and twisted the florescent tube. The tube fell out, and she couldn't get it back in. Then the cover for the light wouldn't hook back on the ceiling.

I said, "Kathy, you can't leave that like that. If it would fall, you could get hurt."

"Well," she said, "then I'll just sue the government for the injuries." The laughter started again.

Visit from Mitch

Mitch came to visit on Saturday, June 4, 1994. His face was stressed with the marks that are noticeable when he is worried. I asked him about how he was feeling.

"This situation is never far from my mind. All the things that have happened to you and you not being responsible for any of it really bother me. I am totally disillusioned with the legal system," he told me.

While we visited, he told me that he was also concerned that someone might try to harm me sexually. He told me that if anything like that would ever happen, do whatever I had to do to stay alive. I certainly hoped nothing like that happened, but I knew that it did happen because I had heard about it.

"Do whatever you have to do to survive, and I'll never blame you for anything. If you have to do something against your morals, put it aside when you walk out the door and never think of it again," he instructed me.

We talked about the things happening in the prison and the things that I saw and experienced. Hopefully, I distracted him from where we were.

"I love you," I told him as I put my arms around him and said goodbye. "I want us to go somewhere for a little while when I get out of here." He would have time during the Fourth of July weekend. I was a little concerned that we might be in the midst of trial preparation, and I might not be able to take enough time to go somewhere.

Strip Search

After Mitch left, I went in to be strip-searched. There were two black women in there at the same time. One of them took off her pants and tossed them at the correctional officer, Puzo. Something fell out of the pants, and I saw it. "Something fell," I said.

There was no response from anyone, and the correctional officer almost stood on it, that's how close it was to her foot. She let those two women out, and I finished putting my clothes on.

"What's this?" she asked as she looked down at the plastic glove laying on the floor.

"It fell out of that woman's pants when she tossed them to you. Didn't you hear me say, 'something fell'?" I answered her.

She picked it up and looked at it. It was a clear plastic glove with white powder in one finger and half of another. Running out to get the women, she was too late. The woman who was to escort me back to the mental health unit was told to take me to the lieutenant's office. She did, and he finally called me in.

Alan Scott was absolutely the most obnoxious person I had ever met. To identify him as "human" was a compliment.

"What's your name?" he snarled.

"Lynn Hartz," I replied.

"What's your number?" he barked.

"04524-088."

"What happened, and what did you see?" he probed in a hateful voice.

I told him what had happened. Then he said, "It wasn't yours?"

"No, I don't do stuff like that."

He said, "How do you know what it is?"

"I don't, but I can make a good guess."

All of a sudden he looked up at me and said, "Get out of here. I'm sick of looking at your face." So the lady who was my escort took me back to the mental health unit. He told the officer that he'd get everyone drug tested.

I told the women about my experience, and they told me that he talked that way to everyone—staff, his bosses, it didn't matter. I can't imagine how or why he kept his job. It has been my experience with men who have a similar attitude that they probably compared themselves in the locker room in high school and realized that they came up short.

The next day I actually saw Payne being compassionate to one of the women. She started crying during lunch, and he took her in his office and talked to her for a long, long time. When I saw her later, she said that she was fine.

I didn't do much the rest of that day except read and watch TV.

When I called Mitch the next evening, he had been worrying over that incident from the previous day. He was afraid that someone would try to kill me, and he constantly worried that I couldn't take care of myself because he wasn't there to protect me. When he became upset, I worried about him having a stroke or a heart attack. Then what would we do? I'd have to take care of him. I prayed that nothing would happen. He kept saying that I was innocent and naive and had no experience dealing with trashy people. He saw the staff as trash, as well as the prisoners.

I continued praying that something would happen to cause his faith to strengthen. I knew what it was like to be angry at God and not even believe that He was omnipotent.

Shake Down

June 5 was a quiet day until the staff pulled a "shake down" in the evening. That is when the staff goes into each person's room, and they go through all of your belongings, personal and otherwise.

"I'm going to write you up for excessive laundry," that nasty nurse, Bobbie, who didn't like me, bellowed. That was the silliest thing I ever heard. Evelyn and I had just taken all of our clean clothes out of the dryer, and I was in our room folding and separating the clothes. She was a most despicable person. Ms. Brown and Payne were with her. They came in the room and told me to leave. They went through every drawer, locker, and shelf. When I was finally allowed back in my room, I couldn't find my cookies, and they had taken my extra pillow. These people were on one power and control trip. They seem to like to play "poleece."

Jackie

One woman who left the prison gave Jackie Wilson her shoes. When they did the "shake down" they took Jackie's shoes, because they hadn't been bought at the commissary. Jackie was a heavyset, light-skinned woman who had no outside support from her family. If she had the shoes on, they would not have taken them. She had been in the mental health unit for fourteen years. She wore T-shirts with holes in them and was quite unkempt. I liked Jackie and would have liked to have done something to help her, but it didn't seem possible. Jackie was in prison for a violent crime. She was quite open, and freely talked about herself and her situation. I asked her if she was schizophrenic when she committed the crime, and she told me that she believed that she was, but that she wasn't anymore, since she was treated medically.

Jackie was certainly not a stupid woman. The guards seemed to like her, and would spend time talking with her. Mr. Payne even helped her find a job so that she could earn a little money while she was there.

I liked Jackie's sense of humor. She wrote to a town close to Lexington that had a problem keeping a mayor. She told them that she had plenty of time to be their mayor, and would be glad to have the job. Jackie said she could even do it from prison, because she didn't have anything else to do! Of course, it was printed in the Lexington newspaper, and people laughed at her. I wondered if the people who laughed understood that she did it as a joke.

Bathing Fran

I was so nervous on Tuesday, June 7, that I could hardly contain myself.

The staff decided to give a woman a bath and force medication on her. Fran came in dirty, grimy, and uncooperative. Seven correctional officers went in the mental health ward to help. They put on their riot squad equipment and were ready for a big hullabaloo. All the rest of the women prisoners stood around watching the goings-on.

"Ms. Ware, have I missed seeing anything while I've been here?" I asked.

She chuckled. "Just the women acting up on the second floor."

"Well, I've seen that in other mental hospitals," I told her.

Fran was compliant and didn't cause any trouble. A couple of days later she said that when she took her medicine she was fine.

Tension was tight as a tightrope. Everyone was edgy.

I talked with Dr. George for about an hour. He was waiting on word from the judge as to how comprehensive of an evaluation he wanted. The law clerk called back while I was there, and the judge wanted it to be comprehensive. Dr. George said that he would not be leaving town until Saturday in order to finish his work before he left.

He asked me if I was competent before the accident, and I told him that I was fine and had worked the day of the accident. Then I helped him get the sequence of events straight, related to the so-called obstruction of justice charge.

I had read all the books that were sent to me. I was not sure what I was going to do with my time. I wanted to go home.

Then I thought about something rather amusing. My bond conditions said that I couldn't have any contact with felons. So, what did they do? They put me in a maximum security prison where all I had for contacts were felons! *What a crazy situation,* I thought.

More Psychological Testing

On Friday, June 10, 1994, Dr. Wright did another test. It was a puzzle test that was done blindfolded. Another test was to read words of colors, red, blue and green. Then I had to say the colors as they appeared and then to say the colors, even when the word would be something else, another color. For example, the word "red" would be written in blue ink. It was very confusing. He said these tests would take an hour, but we were finished in about twenty-five minutes.

As Dr. George was leaving, I asked if I would still be in the prison until he returned. He said that he was leaving Dr. Wright in charge of my study, and he didn't know if there was anything else he needed to do. I told him that Dr. Wright said that he was finished, unless he saw something else on the QEEG (the brain scan) that was important. Dr. George said that he would call and ask him the status of the situation.

When I talked to Carroll, he said that everything was in the Fourth Circuit Court of Appeals, and that on Monday he would call a woman there and try to get the appeal moved along at a rapid pace.

"Counselor Mitch"

When I talked to Mitch, he said that he had spent hours on the telephone with some of my clients. It is unbelievable how some people who need help so badly will share their whole life with anyone.

"I'm going to get my license and start charging!" he laughed.

On Saturday, June 11, 1994, I did nothing until visiting time. Mitch came over and brought Hope and Grace, two of my daughters. I was surprised to see them. I missed my children, and there were things I needed to do for them right then that I couldn't, such as make a dress for Grace for her Rainbow Girls statewide convention. We had a nice time talking. It seemed like such a long time since I had seen them!

Hope said that Shem, my daughter Nell's boyfriend, won one-fourth of $10,000 from a radio station, for a treasure hunt contest. That was really nice! I knew they could use the money.

That time it was more difficult to say goodbye. The injustice of the situation absolutely galled me. There were many times that I felt as though this was all a dream—no, a nightmare—and it wasn't really happening to me. I wondered, *What could happen next?*

After they left, I finished reading a book—470 pages. It was one of the books that Hope had mailed that I finally received.

Sunday morning I got up late. There wasn't anything left to eat. The guard was eating the last of the cinnamon rolls. I had a banana, which Evelyn had saved for me, and some milk, which were hardly adequate for my medicine.

The reason I was late getting up was that I was awakened at 6:00 a.m. for a random urinalysis. I wondered how random it really was, especially after the previous Saturday's episode. The woman guard said that my name "just came up on the computer." Kathy didn't believe it, and neither did I. Although I had nothing to hide, I resented being awakened at 6:00 on Sunday morning and having someone watch me pee. Perhaps I would have felt differently had I been sent to prison for drugs, but why should I be harassed like that? I believed that it was related to the incident the week before.

A lawyer in Lexington, who worked with Carroll's law firm, made a special visit the following Monday. He took my journal in order for me to get it out of prison. All the mail incoming and outgoing was read, and I didn't know if it would make it out if I didn't have it picked up.

On Tuesday, I was informed that I would have a "team" meeting on Wednesday. A team meeting consisted of all of the staff on the mental health unit: the doctors, the recreation director, the activities' director, Mr. Payne, the counselor, and the case manager, whom I had only seen once. The meeting was about as bland as a dry piece of bread. It didn't last very long, and I didn't say very much. What was there to say? Maybe that I had the qualifications to run a prison, and I'd do a heck of a better job?

I picked up the telephone Tuesday evening and called home. Mitch was at my house. One ring. Two rings. "Hello," I began. "Mitch, can you come pick me up Friday morning, by nine o'clock?"

"Are you sure? I thought they were going to keep you until the 29th." Although I had told him over and over that I was not going to be in that prison that long, he didn't believe me.

"I am *sure*. We had a meeting today, and I don't know why they didn't let me go home today, but you need to be here Friday at nine o'clock. Bring me something to wear home," I instructed.

Impatient, I didn't know if I could wait until Friday. Physically, I felt better than I had for a while.

The women who were leaving the prison had to check out on Thursday. I was given a pair of pants and a shirt to wear home. *Ugly* would not begin to describe the outfit. It seemed to take forever to go to all the different places for release, but finally I was through.

Mitch arrived Friday, right on time. He hugged and kissed me, and we walked to the truck. "Did you ever see any clothes any uglier?" I moaned.

He just laughed as I stripped my clothes off with a vengeance right there in the parking lot, and I changed into the blouse and skirt he had brought.

It had been the longest month of my life, and I was *finally* going home.

Whatever will come next cannot be as bad as this, I thought. I was still irate.

Chapter 4

How to Lose a Legal Case

"So, you went home then. What happened next?" Lady Di paused. But before I could respond, she continued, "You know. I spent time in Lexington, too. I'll have to tell you about it sometime."

"Well, I went home, and Mitch and I went on a short vacation," I told her. "We went to Williamsburg, Virginia, and had a really pleasant few days. Nothing much happened with my case for several weeks. Every once in a while I would need to meet with the lawyers, but a court date hadn't even been set yet. Actually, there wasn't even a report from the competency exam for about a month. I would be calm sometimes, then frustrated with the situation, and anxious at other times."

"That sounds like me, too," Lady Di affirmed, as she worked on her fingernails.

Competency Evaluation

The competency evaluation was everything that I expected it to be—a farce. It was full of mistakes and innuendos.

The report sounded like I was a snobbish, arrogant, self-centered individual, which is the antithesis of the kind of person that I am. Most people see me as a warm, kind, giving individual who usually thinks of others before she thinks of herself. The local television and radio interviews, the government publications that were written about me, and the local newspaper reports had always described me as just the opposite. Those documents had always portrayed me as a person rising above my roots, seeing all people as deserving of the same rights and opportunities, and always willing to lend a helping hand.

I had worked for Purdue University in the early 1960's, and I had made a comment to one of the doctors about the attitude of the men working at Purdue. They discriminated against women for promotions, and attempted to terminate women for various reasons that were not even job-related. My statement about that was accurate, because there were no laws or legislation to protect women in the workplace from such discrimination. Dr. George alluded to my tendencies to "paranoia," using this as an example. Perhaps he lived under a rock during the sixties, but this kind of discrimination toward women existed more intensely then than it does now.

I had told Dr. George that I had dated my husband, Bill, from the age of fifteen, when I was in high school, through college until we were twenty-four, then we married after we reunited at the University of Arizona campus. Again, Dr. George made it sound as though my relationship with Bill had just been casual dating, and that I had married on the spur of the moment. That was not true. We had a "lover's quarrel," and didn't see each other for about a year. Then we encountered each other on the campus of the University of Arizona on February 29, 1968, Leap Year day. Bill and I knew that we were supposed to be together. Why would a professional psychologist distort such information? I have yet to believe it to be anything more than disregard for the truth and an unwillingness to see incarcerated people as human beings.

There were other allegations related to my social security claim that was pending and my unwillingness to be taken outside the prison in handcuffs and chains for the EEG and a CAT scan. Even as I write this, I still feel enraged about the court's power to send someone to prison before a conviction of a crime. It made sense to me to use a psychological report for two different purposes. Why not? And if I caused problems for the staff at the hospital because I refused to be taken out in handcuffs and chains, then I'm glad. If I caused a disturbance, then I'm glad. I'm glad because my behavior forced them to see me as a person, not as a piece of property that they could ignore.

Of course, I was found to be competent. I had never said that I wasn't, only that I had a problem with memory and other types of distortions. I still suffer with some of the memory problems and some dyslexia related to numerals.

When I returned to West Virginia, I went to see Dr. Whelan, my personal psychiatrist. I told him that I was having more problems with memory than I did previously. When I would see people, they would all look like someone from the prison. Also, numbers would flip-flop. For example, a six would look like a nine, and a one would look like a seven. He told me that condition is called "Ganser's Syndrome." It is called "the syndrome of approximations," and usually affects people in prison. It used to be called the "prison syndrome," and stress is usually the cause. When I am very tired or feel stressed, I still have to be cautious with balancing a checkbook, and people still look like someone from the prison. Being in the prison made my psychological health worse.

Pre-Trial Motions

Pretrial motions are simply rules that the prosecution and defense lawyers present to the judge for him to determine certain procedures in the actual trial. Needless to say, everything that was presented by my defense attorneys was denied.

One motion was to limit certain types of information, such as bringing up billing that had happened before dates of the indicted offenses.

When Will was still my lawyer, we had entered pre-trial motions; then, when he was dismissed from my case, all that work had to be done again. It is extremely important to note that *I was denied the right to counsel of my choice*. I believed then, and I believe now, that my constitutional rights were violated, especially when the reason for which I was denied my counsel of choice (he could be a witness against me in the "obstruction of justice" charge) was never pursued by the prosecutor. Someone wanted Will off my case, and it wasn't me.

Carroll submitted the same, or similar, motions as Will. One was to dismiss two of the charges, one was to limit evidence, and another was on entrapment. When these were submitted, the judge considered them "under protest," because Carroll had not submitted them in a timely matter. I think that the tardiness of his work had a great influence on judges' decision to deny the motions. If I were the judge, I would have been irritated that this was not done promptly. Perhaps this influenced the judge negatively.

Will had submitted a motion to require the prosecutors to disclose exculpatory evidence, but that didn't come up in the new pre-trial motions. For anyone who might not understand the legal term "exculpate," it means anything that would vindicate a person from wrongdoing. Legal vocabulary is used as a means of intimidating the public, and making the legal profession appear "superior" and "beyond reach" to non-lawyers. It really isn't, once you learn new definitions and lingo.

Another motion that was presented was that I had been "entrapped." I asserted that I did nothing different with the people who pretended to be clients than with normal clients. We did not use that motion.

Carroll continually told me that he was friendly with the prosecutor, but he certainly didn't use his relationship to make the situation more amenable. The only major item that was agreed upon was a *voir dire* for each prospective juror. A *voir dire* is a questionnaire given to each person about various things, such as their contact with me, Blue Cross, their type of work, etc.

Lawyers' Strategies

I thought that my lawyers had a strategy, but as I reflect on it, I do not think that they did. They had a large chart made that showed all of the activity related to Blue Cross, my business, the investigators, and the U.S. Attorney's office. But THEY NEVER USED IT!

My lawyers had a list of witnesses that were notified that they would be asked to testify, and the government was to pay their costs, BUT THEY NEVER USED THEM, EITHER!

During the last week before the trial, I expected to meet with the lawyers every day, but I had to call them, and when I did, they told me they didn't need to meet with me. I was not kept informed as to what they were doing and planning.

"You Confessed"

My problem had been only with Blue Cross and Blue Shield of Southern W.Va. No problem existed with any other company. I could not understand what the problem was and, to this day, I still don't.

In 1982 the vice-president of Blue Cross, Mr. Edgar Estill, came to my office to see me. He thought that I needed assistance with billing their company, which I did. My business was new, and the practice of counseling was not approved as a provider, but I was permitted to sign for whatever a psychologist was allowed to sign. None of the people working in my office knew anything about billing codes or procedure codes. That was not taught in graduate school at that time. (It is taught now.) So Mr. Estill taught me the billing codes, procedure codes, and how to set up a sliding fee scale for those people who did not have insurance to help defray the costs of their treatment. He also told me to write in the amount of time in hours, minutes, or both when using a code for billing groups. We were not being paid adequately for group work. Psychotherapy is a time-dependent treatment, unlike other types of medical treatment.

Most of what Mr. Estill taught me was the information and billing procedures that were, and still are, used by the mental health centers in our areas, and probably throughout this country. When mental health centers were established twenty-five years ago, psychiatrists were attached to them, either as staff persons or contract workers, for the sole purpose of providing prescription drugs and rendering services for billing insurance companies. I simply did the same thing that the mental health centers were doing, only on a smaller scale.

Almost without exception, all other psychologists and counselors in private practice were billing in the same or similar manner. None of them were investigated. I was a female who was extremely visible to the public. (I had my own local TV program, a radio program, and many articles about my business in the newspaper.) Someone wanted me out of business, and, even though I had already quit because of my injuries, that wasn't enough.

Blue Cross did not have any established procedures or guidelines concerning their preferred provider relations or policies with their doctors. They did not have any written manual on such policies and procedures!

Blue Cross stopped paying my claims. I tried internal procedures and did not get any answers, so I contacted the West Virginia State Insurance Commissioner. Blue Cross refused to answer the complaint, and never paid for the services that had been provided. I was operating a very small business, and depended on reimbursement to exist. That is when they decided to put a "sting" in my office.

Up until this time, I thought that my relationship with Blue Cross was good. I provided free workshops for their staff at their request, and saw many Blue Cross employees as clients. I always accepted what Blue Cross allowed as payment for their employees' insurance as "payment in full" for services rendered. Why they decided not to pay me, I never understood.

I do not know if Blue Cross had a provider relations division before my contact with Mr. Estill, but my office would call provider relations to get information about the individual's insurance reimbursement for mental and nervous conditions. They told us if it was a requirement to have a medical doctor sign the forms. Mr. Estill said that having a medical doctor sign the forms was a carry-over from when only physicians were health providers. A later conversation with Mr. Gerald Nelson, the former director of provider relations, revealed that this was Blue Cross' way of getting around their own internal problem. There never were any established procedures or guidelines concerning if a medical doctor even needed to have face to face contact with the patient. Blue Cross did not have a written manual on such policies and procedures!

Once the federal investigation began, I decided that I would no longer accept Blue Cross/Blue Shield. However, I received a telephone call from the Employee Assistance Program director for the Secret Service in Washington, D.C., asking if I would be willing to see a couple for counseling related to a marital problem. As she explained the situation, I questioned the legitimacy of the call, thinking it might be a set-up to get me to do something wrong. As it turned out, it was a legitimate call. I worked with the couple, their problem was resolved, and I was paid for the services by Blue Cross.

A little later, I had another couple come for counseling, and the husband was a federal employee. I did not see them together, except for thirty minutes on one occasion. All of the charges were billed. All of the charges were legitimate charges, but Blue Cross refused to pay, saying that what I did was marital counseling, and they didn't pay for marital counseling. The billings were exactly the way Mr. Estill had taught me. Mr. Estill told me that all counseling was psychotherapy, and there was no difference, except that psychotherapy was a medical term, and the only one accepted for medical procedures. Logically, how could a therapist do marital counseling with only one person?

Hoping to resolve the problem, I talked to people in provider relations, which was practically nonexistent, because Blue Cross had merged with another Blue Cross. I wrote letters to their review person, who was a nurse. I even wrote to the new President of Blue Cross, a Mr. Ted Ferrell. He never replied to any of my letters or telephone calls. Finally, I contacted the Insurance Commissioner for the State of West Virginia, and filed a complaint. Blue Cross would not answer the complaint, and they never paid that and another claim. It is important to remember that mine was a very small business, which was dependent on reimbursements to exist.

This area had two different Blue Cross companies, one called

Blue Cross/Blue Shield of Southern West Virginia, and the other Blue Cross/Blue Shield of Parkersburg. During the 1970's and early 1980's, there was no licensing law for counselors or social workers in West Virginia. I completed a Ph.D., including an internship, and wanted privileges to sign for insurances for services provided. Blue Cross allowed me that privilege and the Parkersburg people were extremely gracious about it. However, after the merger, the new, merged Blue Cross acted as though it had never heard of me.

All of this time I used a consulting psychiatrist or medical doctor to sign insurance forms for Blue Cross. There always seemed to be a problem keeping a doctor. Some of it had to do with professional competition. At one point I called Provider Relations at Blue Cross and talked with one of the women there about this problem. She told me that I could not use the doctors I had been using, because they were not psychiatrists. This was the very same person who had told me that it would be all right to use a non psychiatrist. So that meant I had to find another doctor.

The new doctor proved to be more of a problem than any doctor that I previously used. We finally agreed that the situation was untenable, which left me without a doctor again.

I called Provider Relations to discuss the problem with them. "Just pick one," the woman told me. "It doesn't matter. Just pick one, and use that one."

"Which one?" I asked. First, they told me I couldn't use one group, and now they were telling me something else.

"Just use the last one you had." She sounded impatient. The last one I had was the one who was trouble. Every time he had been to my office to see patients, he would either call or write me a letter containing comments about his work and the patients. Nothing we did pleased him. He was critical, judgmental, and never had a complimentary thing to say about anything that we did. Instead of reading the work that we had provided, which is what a consultant should do, he "redid" any work that our staff had already done. He did that in order to spend more time in our office and bill my business for more of his services.

"Well, how often does the doctor have to see the patient?" I asked Blue Cross.

"It doesn't matter. You're the boss. It's up to you. He doesn't have to see them at all." I knew that was true, because I knew a doctor in Huntington who allowed a counselor to sign his name to the forms, whether he saw the patient or not. At the trial, this same woman denied that she ever said that, and she added that she was sure I had been forging the doctor's name. The doctors in the group's practice said that they didn't know that their names were used, even though they had seen the patients, signed the original insurance forms, and met with me about the situation. They also received mail at my office, which we hand delivered to them. It is my observation that people will say whatever they believe is necessary to protect themselves, even if it isn't the truth, and other people will believe them, especially if the government is asking questions.

At one time I asked Provider Relations exactly how they wanted the doctor's name to be signed. I was told there were three ways I could do it. "You can sign the doctor's name, you can sign the doctor's name and initial it, or you can use a rubber signature stamp." Never once did they tell me to have the doctor sign his own name.

At one time I talked with the federal investigators and told them the whole story of how Blue Cross told me what to do and how to do it. I had to provide handwriting specimens, even though I told them which forms I had signed. I told them how and why. Then, all these many years later, the lawyers told me that I confessed.

"What do you mean, I confessed?" I practically shouted at them. "I told them what I did, and how I was instructed by Blue Cross to do what I did, and there was a lawyer with me at the time. Will was there. If I had done anything wrong, he would have told me!" The two lawyers looked at each other, then they told me that they wanted me to plead guilty.

"Wait a minute!" I blurted. "I am not guilty of doing anything but following Blue Cross's instructions, but if you think I am, how can you defend me?" They told me that they would defend me anyway. All they had concentrated on was the "sting" that Blue Cross had planted in my office.

Blue Cross had nothing to pursue, and they and the federal prosecutors let my case lay dormant for three months less than five years. A case must be prosecuted or dropped within five years. So, in 1991 Blue Cross put a "sting" in my office.

Two Blue Cross investigators posing as a couple wanting counseling came to my office. I was at home because I had laryngitis and bronchitis and was unable to work, so another woman from my office saw them. However, they were insistent about seeing me, and I agreed to meet with them. The things I was told led me to believe that each of them had a problem of an individual nature, which was causing a relationship problem.

Then, they had another investigator make an appointment and pretend he was having a problem with his weight. He didn't have a diagnostic problem with weight, but everything he told me pointed to depression. My training taught me that if I were ever suspicious of something or someone, to handle everything with the same skills, knowledge, and trust in my professional abilities.

I wasn't suspicious of anything, but my office manager was. When we billed Blue Cross for their services and my name was signed as the provider, the claim came back saying that it needed to have a medical doctor to sign it. She called the alleged couple and was told that the insurance company must have made a mistake because the company that he worked for was new and had just bought insurance, and they would have to call Blue Cross and get it adjusted. That was done, and my company was paid for the services provided. I didn't think anything about it because I was told that they were moving back to Cleveland.

I provided non-traditional therapy with the couple, and even gave the investigator some handouts on weight loss procedures. Even though I did nothing wrong with any of these people, they accused me of false diagnosis and false treatment of my patients. Later, in the appeal, the appellate court said that I did not do false diagnosis or treatment, but that I had no right to *sign my own name* to those forms!

So, I went to trial with two lawyers who believed I was guilty of something, which I knew beyond a shadow of a doubt that I was not. I did not feel good about this at all. In fact, I felt doomed.

The Jury

A jury is supposed to be "of your peers." At least that is what I had always believed. A jury is supposed to be made up of people who are like you. Well, that is not the way juries are constructed. A pool of jurists is given to the court, and the selection is made from those people. There were about thirty from whom to select. There was not one person selected for the jury that was in a field that even resembled mine. Most of them were very undereducated.

The prosecutor eliminated one, then the defense eliminated one. The prosecutor eliminated all of the people who had any education. Even after the jury panel was questioned about their beliefs and prejudices, I did not think that we had a good representation of jurists. There was no one in a profession even similar to mine, no one who even knew anything about the psychiatric field, and no one who looked on me favorably.

Since I experienced this situation with jury selection, I have read about various proposals for juries. Some proposals would have permanent jurists who specialize in such things as medical awards, malpractice, or other such particular conditions. Great Britain uses a similar system now, I understand. It makes more sense than people with little or no information about such situations. I would certainly advocate jury reform.

The Trial

One thing that Carroll did get was the right to have an expert witness related to the billings for Blue Cross. We found Jamie Sullivan (no relation to Will). Carroll submitted a motion, then didn't get a letter to her detailing what he wanted until October 20, 1994. The trial was to be held on October 24, just four days later. Jamie's report was detailed and quite lengthy. She was licensed as an insurance agent to sell life, accident, health, and casualty insurance. She had also been certified in coding and terminology through Blue Cross/ Blue Shield, and was a registered health underwriter for Blue Cross. However, after Carroll hired her, the judge refused to allow her to appear as an expert witness. Because she was not a lawyer, he would not permit her to testify and give a "legal opinion."

The trial lasted for two days. The newspaper and television reporters followed me around. Pictures that they plastered in the newspaper and on the television made me look really bad. All of my illnesses, stress, and pain came through the photographers' cameras, as though that were their main intent.

Prosecutors get the first word and the last word in a trial. That doesn't seem fair to me. I believe the defense should have the last word.

As I reflect on the trial, I feel angry about the lies that were told by one woman who had been employed by me. She was very difficult to have as an employee, and was always and forever saying "I'm sorry." Eventually she decided that she wasn't going to work anymore, and I was glad. She made an issue out of her religious beliefs, constantly said that she didn't lie, and she did everything except tell the truth when she got on the witness stand. The arrangements that we had with all of the doctors were known by her, yet she said that she knew nothing about them. My lawyers did not even confront her with the fact that she made the appointments with the doctors, scheduled the patients, took the files to them, and then picked the files up later the following day. She knew that the doctors knew the billing arrangement, because she sat next to me while I talked with their office manager on the telephone and told her exactly what I needed.

The doctors' office manager and the doctors did not admit knowledge of these arrangements, either. Yet I had a letter that was used as documentation, telling the doctors that Blue Cross would no longer allow me to use their services for billing.

After the prosecutors used all their witnesses, my lawyers decided that they had not proved their case, and we didn't need to call any witnesses. They had several people waiting for notification to come to West Virginia as our witnesses. But the lawyers decided not to use them.

I knew I was doomed. My intuition proved to be correct.

The Verdict

The jury deliberated for four hours. One of my lawyers speculated that there might be a split decision. When we were called at their office, it was 8:30 p.m. Across the street, my whole family was waiting in the court room. All of my brothers and sisters, my daughters, and some of my cousins, nieces, and nephews were there. There were also all the people from the U.S. Attorney's Office, the public defender's office, the media, and some people who were there for voyeuristic purposes.

The judge had all of the jurors stand in front of him in a semicircle. The jury foreman handed him the verdict, and I had to stand while he read each charge separately. I was found guilty of all seven charges.

I was taken upstairs, where I was fingerprinted and photographed again. The judge allowed me to stay at home on a bond, pending the sentencing.

The Sentencing

A pre-sentence report was prepared by a woman who was a probation officer. She made the report sound worse than the competency evaluation. She enhanced the guidelines which we protested in the sentencing, and the judge made a compromise. Not that it did much good.

Sentencing took two days because the prosecutor tried to say that

I owed Blue Cross $32,000. This was absolutely not true, but the judge upheld the amount. However, he said that since Blue Cross had filed bankruptcy, and so had I, all I had to pay back was $737.50, plus $350 in court costs. I was going to prison for 21 months, which meant I would spend a total of eighteen months in confinement.

I was going to prison, and was sentenced to more time than anyone expected. I kept telling myself. *I didn't do it! It isn't fair! How could God let this happen to me?* I was infuriated, outraged, and hostile because this happened to me.

In Summary

It's easy to lose a case like this. First, follow directions of those in authority. Second, be denied your counsel of choice. Third, be appointed lawyers who don't know anything about criminal law, insurance, or mental health procedures. Fourth, have lawyers who refuse to use any witnesses. Fifth, have witnesses that were approved be denied by the court. Finally, have a lawyer who doesn't speak loudly enough to be heard or have any effective public speaking skills, and a judge who appears to have animosity toward you.

Someone wanted me convicted of a crime. I was never given a warning or a reprimand or even told I did anything wrong. These procedures had been used locally for twenty-five years, and I had operated my business in a similar manner for seventeen years.

The only option I was even given was to plead guilty to a felony. That would have kept me out of prison, but I could never have an appeal, and I still would have lost my licenses to practice. I tried that, and the judge said I didn't believe I did anything wrong, so he refused the plea.

I believe that "winning" is more important to the prosecution than "truth." Gerry Spence, the well-known criminal defense attorney who has never lost a case, has said over and over that it is almost impossible to beat the government, because they have all the power. The above conditions made me a powerless victim of uncontrollable circumstances.

Feeling empty and spiritually abandoned, I went to the little twenty-four-hour chapel next to the hospital. There was only a little comfort there.

Chapter 5

Going to the Chapel

February 22, 1995
Dear Mitch,

...Oh, let me tell you about church. I have never had such a wonderful church experience, ever. The gal that plays the piano is an inmate from Nashville and a professional musician. I could never play the way she does. But that is beside the point. Remember, there are a lot of black women here and they go to church. Believe me, they go to church and they sing, and believe me, they sing! Can you imagine what it's like to be one of only a few white women in a church packed with singing black women? That church has more spirit in it than any church I have ever been to in my life! The chaplain spoke about Samuel hearing the voice of God at night and not knowing whose voice he was hearing. It was a dynamic presentation. It was certainly like no other church service I have ever been to and they didn't even pass a collection plate!

Now, let me tell you something else. This land may be the property of the federals, but I learned that in God's eyes, the place is God's land. I learned that by what I feel walking around here. It feels good to touch God's mountaintop in West Virginia. It is still God's land. The robins, the squirrels, the crows—they are right here! I'll bet at some place there are deer, too . . .

The chapel was the first place I wanted to go.

The chaplains were supposed to allow religious items to be sent in for the inmate, which were not supposed to count against allowed personal items, which could only be sent in twice a year.

I wrote Mitch on March 1, 1995 requesting that he send in my personal religious items and telling him how mail it into the chaplain.

I told him that the mail room would not open it because it would be addressed to the chaplain. I wanted my necklace, which was broken. I had the necklace made and Mitch had one exactly like it, only slightly larger. It was an Indian Medicine Wheel, with stones for each of the colors of the four directions, with a star of David and a cross in the middle of it. There were four feathers hanging from the bottom of the medicine wheel. I asked him to put the feather back on my necklace and mail it in the same box. It was valuable, but I wanted it because I was emotionally attached to it, and I felt like something was missing.

The list also included the case that all my religious items were in as well as my Indian cards, Medicine Woman cards, Medicine Cards and Books (animals), Sacred Path cards and Book, *Story of Unity* book, Ko-Lam-Ni book (about hands on healing), *Guidepost* Parallel Bible, angel cards, and *The Medium, The Mystic and the Physicist* (a hardback book by LaShan).

The chaplain told me that the package had been authorized, but it was returned to Mitch by the mail room, saying that it was unauthorized. That meant I had to verify the authorization through the chapel, and then have Mitch mail the package back. The staff in R&D insisted that they did not have the authorization, and the chapel workers were just as insistent that they had sent it. I finally received the package.

Mitch did not send me my necklace, because he was afraid that someone would steal it. He was unable to find a couple of the books that I wanted, too. But the important things were there.

My Argument with God

I had a continual argument with God. This argument had been going on since the indictments. In April 1995 I wrote to Mitch about it.

> *Yesterday, I had an argument with God, Himself. I told Him that enough was enough, and I want to go home where I belong. I had an argument with Him about healing some people here and teaching anyone else anything else. I was tired of being used, even by Him, and I want Him to stop putting pressure on me. I've had enough!*
>
> *His answer was to heal three people and teach one, and I'd be done. I argued with Him about the healing. He doesn't need me to do it. I told Him I didn't think I could do it, and He asked me whom I thought I was. When He told me to do something, I didn't do it alone, and I knew that.*
>
> *Anyway, I guess I am feeling that all I've ever tried to do was God's work, and all He wants to do is to use me, and I want some joy, peace and happiness, and He hasn't even provided that for me for very long at a time. I am going to ask for that from now on, and tell Him that I deserve it.*
>
> *...I don't think I'm finished (with my argument) yet. He (God) can get someone else to do His work. I am really mad. If He is a protective, loving God, why did He allow this to happen to me? I am tired of people saying things like, "You'll know at a later time." HE needs to tell me NOW!*

But I still had no answers as to "why."

Chaplains and the Chapel Staff

The inmates who worked in the chapel were a clique. There was supposed to be an equal representation of blacks, whites and Spanish, as well as an equitable distribution of Christians, Jews, and Moslems. There were a few other religious groups represented in the prison, but so few that they did not make an impact on chapel politics.

When I first went to the prison, there were two chaplains: a woman, Chaplain Sweet, who dressed very masculinely and was heavy built; and a man, Larry Short, who was a fundamental Christian and a Navy Chaplain. Chaplain Sweet seemed nice to those who were able to get to talk with her, but it seemed that only a few were able to do that. She was very friendly with the inmate who played the piano and another woman. They were in her office having a conference every time I wanted to ask a simple question. Chaplain Sweet spoke once, and I was impressed with her message about "Listening to the Voice of God." Within two months after I arrived, Chaplain Sweet transferred to a men's maximum security prison as the head chaplain.

Chaplain Larry Short thought his beliefs were the only beliefs, and if you did not believe his way, then you were doomed to eternal damnation. He definitely did not like me and my "off-brand" religion. He did not seem too happy when I pointed out to him that there would be no daily devotional guide in the prison if it wasn't for my religion

Perhaps I need to mention that I belong to Unity, which is headquartered in Lee's Summit, Missouri. Unity publishes the popular *Daily Word,* which is a monthly devotional. It was provided free to inmates in most prisons in the United States, as well as some outside of the United States.

Chaplain Short could not argue with that, but he did not like it that I had my religious items sent in through the chapel, and included in it my animal cards, Native American cards, and the sacred path cards. However, by policy, he had to honor my request.

I would like to say that when I use any tool, such as the cards, I always pray that my eyes be open to whatever message God wants me to see, and that He let me know if I am to share that information with anyone. At times I am given very specific visions, and at other times just sketchy information. There are seldom any situations that

I do not share with the people who are asking, but God directs me to always use wisdom. I might also point out that I do not need any "tool" to "know things." However, most people expect you to use a "tool," and find it interesting. It makes my work easier, so I willingly oblige.

Mitch Visits the Chapel

"Do you want to come visit for Easter Sunday and go to the chapel service and eat dinner with us?" I asked Mitch when I called him a few weeks before Easter. The notice about the special visit had just been posted on the bulletin board, and I was sure that he would feel better if he could walk around the grounds and eat in the cafeteria.

"Are you sure about this?" He was surprised that such a visit would be permitted. After all, his only experience with the federal prison system was what I had endured in Lexington.

"Positive," I affirmed. "I have to make reservations. You need to be here at 10:30 that morning so we can go to the chapel, and then go to dinner. It will cost you $2.50 for dinner, and you pay it when you arrive to visit."

Mitch had no idea what to expect. I had told him about the chapel, but by the time he visited, the woman chaplain had been transferred, and the man was on active duty for a while. A visiting black woman pastor spoke that day, as well as a black man. These people drove to Alderson one a month from Washington, D.C. and traveled to other prisons on the other weekends. The significance of her being black was that she attracted the black inmates, and the chapel was full. The prison choir was mostly black women with a few Spanish women as members.

The singing was loud, and I played the piano. The choir, led by Christ Barrett, one of the women I knew from food services, sang *a cappella*. Chris was a dynamic director, and pulled music out of those women that sounded like Sidney Poitier directing the nuns to sing "Amen," in the movie, *Lilies of the Field*. I believe that people sing during times of adversity, because singing heals the wounded soul, as one old song confirms.

Dinner was wonderful. There were tablecloths on the tables and flowers in vases in the center of each. The food was excellent, as well as plentiful. Ham and turkey were both served with all of the trimmings, as well as pies and beverages. Mitch always ate too much, and this was no exception. I thought that he was most impressed with the food, but months later he still talked about the chapel service and the black women singing.

Church at Home

10 April 1995

At church on April 2, I played Pontius Pilate in a soliloquy. It was called "Lonely at the Top," and was a modern expression of his agony when visited by a "lobbyist" he had helped the previous Friday, by crucifying their enemy. Set on Easter Sunday, he couldn't imagine what they could want that couldn't wait until Monday. I really enjoyed doing this play... (Letter from my brother, Andy.)

How I wished I could have seen it. Andy and his sons really enjoyed participating in their church plays. Andy's wife, Sharon, usually worked with the music, because she played the piano for children's church.

I missed my own church, too, and those wonderful friends who are there in times of need. I had taken one address with me when I left—Peg Garrett's—and I wrote her as soon as I could. I knew that Peg had many responsibilities caring for her ill husband. I didn't expect her to write frequently. She shared my letter with the people in my church, so they could write to me.

How blessed I was to have Sylvia Kelly write to me as frequently as she did. The first letter she sent she included a tape, and it was returned to her. She thought: *Oops! What have I done wrong*? She had no idea that a tape couldn't be mailed into the prison.

Sylvia and I have always had a mutual interest in psychic phenomena, and she mentioned a new program that was on television called "The Other Side," which was hosted by Will Miller. I watched it before I went to the prison. My fondest memories of letters from Sylvia always mentioned the church, and people that I cared about, as well as an occasional program of church events. We shared many things, but she continually encouraged me. "I hope you are out sooner than you think. I am imagining you smiling and walking out the prison door waving goodbye. I am also imagining you smiling throughout the day while there, and being as happy as you can."

The word for Sylvia's letters was "encouragement." She could give lessons in how to be an encourager. Even in the midst of her own circumstances, with retirement and problems with her family, she still took time for me.

"All is Not Healthy"

To say that there were problems with the chapel would be an understatement. The problems were the *chaplains.* Chaplain Sweet was gone, leaving Chaplain Short in charge. As I mentioned previously, he was dogmatic about his beliefs, which caused him to play favorites with the inmates. But as I would talk with various inmates, that is not all that he played with them!

"He felt my leg," one woman told me.

"I filed a complaint about him, and no one ever did anything," another woman said.

Anyone who knows anything about how government works, knows that it moves slowly. And that is exactly what happened with the problem with Chaplain Short. The problem, however, grew bigger and bigger. One day Chaplain Short was gone, without any explanation. He was not even allowed back on the prison grounds. Someone else cleaned out his desk. The rumors were rampant.

An odd thing about rumors in prison is that they are almost always accurate. The inmates were told that Chaplain Short had returned to active due in the navy, but there wasn't a woman there who believed anything except that he had been fired for cause, and the "cause" was probably related to sexual harassment.

It was a long time before the prison had another full-time chaplain. The month before I left, an Episcopalian female priest, Nora Wilson, was appointed the new chaplain. She was the first female Episcopalian priest to be appointed as chaplain in any federal prison. I could tell by looking at her that she would do well with the women. She had a motherly appearance and a kind face. Although she seemed to distance herself in early introductions to people, I felt that it was perhaps personal shyness. Because I was leaving, and I knew that these women needed God's love to shine through her, I prayed for this new chaplain.

The Radio Minister

"Did you hear the letter that was read from Sally Jo?" I overheard one of the young inmates asking another. The young inmate, Cara Roberts, was a pretty, light-skinned black girl who had leukemia. She had just been diagnosed with it when she was processed in prison.

"Who is Sally Jo?" the other gal asked Cara.

"I don't know, but she knows me, and requested prayer for me."

I was working in the kitchen with these women, and we were putting silverware away. "Cara, who do you think Sally Jo is?" I asked.

Her beautiful eyes widened a little. "I don't have any idea, but she knows everything going on here. Why wouldn't she use her real name?"

I looked at her and laughed. "Because I'm Sally Jo, and I am from this area, and I simply do not want my name used on the air so that I can be identified."

"You're Sally Jo!" They both laughed as they hugged me. "We should have guessed, because you care enough to do something like that."

Jim Franklin's radio ministry was a highlight of many of the women's week. He had three radio shows a week in the West Virginia area, but we could only get one of them consistently every week and maybe the Sunday morning show, if the atmosphere was right.

Jim read letters from people, prayed, and played gospel music. It had a real "homey" feel to it. People that I didn't know listened to it. I thought that writing to him would be a good way to get information out to the public about the people in the prison, and what life in the prison was like. It worked. He read every letter that I ever sent. I would capsulize the week's events in the prison, and then I would request prayer for the people that I knew who were sick or discouraged.

When some of the women found out that I wrote the letters, they began to ask me to request prayer for them, or to share something with Rev. Franklin. I encouraged them to write to him and tell him themselves, but, as I soon discovered, there were many who just wouldn't do it.

I continued writing to Rev. Franklin when I went to the halfway house, but when I went home, I could no longer get the program clearly enough to listen. I shared so much with the listeners, and learned from them, too.

Many were housebound, confined by a bed or a wheelchair. I began to know these people, because they were more "in prison" than I was.

A Visit from A.R.E.

The Association for Research and Enlightenment interested me for many, many years. It is the organization that was founded by Edgar Cayce, probably the greatest modern prophet of all times. For more than twenty years, I wanted to go to Virginia Beach to the building where the foundation is housed and attend workshops. Who would ever believe that I would have the opportunity to hear a speaker from A.R.E. while I was in prison?

But that is exactly what happened.

It took a petition to the warden, but those women who were interested in metaphysics, which is just another word for spirituality, were neglected by many or all of the activities in the chapel program. Actually, Chaplain Short totally ignored any requests from the inmates for programs of a metaphysical or mystical nature. My friend, Donna Hawthorne, drafted the petition and had interested inmates sign it. Then she submitted it to the warden. He was totally uninformed about anything related to metaphysical or spiritual programs, and had to research some things through the Bureau of Prisons.

There were programs such as those that had been requested in other prisons, and some of them were very strong programs. He approved the programs, and a woman from A.R.E. was contacted.

Miriam Puryear came to the prison for a presentation in March. She had worked for A.R.E. for about thirty years and had written several books. Although she said that she was more than sixty years old, she did not wear glasses for any purpose. Her weight was normal, and she had no health problems.

The room where she spoke was packed, and people were standing around the walls. Those who stood were correctional officers who were interested, as well as prisoners who did not arrive early enough to find seats.

That was only the beginning. I received a note from Donna a year after I left the prison thanking me for helping them with books and material that was sent in through my church at a later date.

Sweat Lodge

Another experience that I wanted to participate in and had never had the opportunity was an American Indian Sweat Lodge Ceremony.

"Let me know the next time you are going to have a sweat lodge. I'd really like to participate," I told Evie Jordan, the spiritual leader of the American Indian women in the prison. There were not very many Indian women in prison at Alderson, because most of the Indian women were from the western United States. However, Evie was from the northeast, probably Iroquois. She had been in prison for a long time. She had a ten-year sentence for drug conspiracy.

A few weeks later Evie asked, "Do you want to do a 'sweat' with us this weekend?"

"Oh, yes! Thanks for asking me!" I called home and told my family and Mitch not to plan to visit me on Saturday. I'm sure they thought that my mind was addled by this request. I didn't think Mitch would think that, but the rest of my family might.

Evie was allowed to drive on the prison ground, because she worked for grounds maintenance. She had the truck and all of the items that were needed for the construction of the sweat lodge. That included everything except the poles, because the poles were permanent and already set in place. There was wood for the fire, blankets to cover the lodge, and canvas to cover the blankets. There were also food and water provided by the food service for nourishment after the sweat.

A sweat lodge is built from right to left, and everything must be done in a circle moving from right to left. First, we covered the poles with the blankets, then placed the blankets on the ground, leaving room in the center for the stones.

It was an eclectic group that participated that day! Evie, an Indian woman, another Indian woman, a Chinese woman, a Black woman, a Spanish woman, and me. Each of us crawled into the lodge on our hands and knees. I quickly realized that I was still unable to put any pressure on my knee as a result of the surgery from the wreck. So I compensated by using my arms to lift my body, instead of my knees.

As the heat intensified, a couple of the women took off some of their clothing. I didn't at first, but the hotter it became, the more I decided to take off.

A sweat lodge is a sacred place to pray. The steam heat is a purification process, cleansing both the body and the spirit. We prayed together for many things. The Chinese woman had never prayed before, so the experience was entirely new to her. With every round of prayers, water was added to the bricks, making the temperature rise.

Prayers were for families, women in prisons, world conditions, problems at the prison, for changes in our country's legal system, and for health, strength and perseverance for all who were incarcerated.

Two of us became too hot, just before the last round of prayers, and we had to exit the sweat lodge. I was disappointed in myself that I "couldn't handle the heat."

But I learned so much that day from Evie. She put her whole self into the experience of sharing and teaching us. The joy I felt of being cleansed and purified was an experience that I will never forget.

And I thought, *Who would ever have guessed that I would have an opportunity to experience this in a prison?*

Finally, I wasn't quite as angry at God as I had been. I was learning that "He can make anything beautiful in your life."

Perhaps I was a little slow in learning this, but I was now sure of it.

Chapter 6

What's up, Doc?

Health Services

Health service was very active with the inmate population. If an inmate was sick, one of the doctors or physician assistants would give her an "idle" for the length of time that she would be unable to work. They also handled routine health care and specialized services, such as what was provided by a hospital outside of the prison. If it was needed, an inmate driver would take an inmate to the clinic or hospital for the service needed. On specific occasions, where an inmate might not be classified as "community custody," a correctional officer was the escort. However, the women were never escorted to the hospital or clinic in handcuffs or chains, and were always treated with the utmost respect and dignity.

My first experience with health services was with Dr. Williams. Jane Flowers, a professional friend of mine for more than twenty years, knew him because they served on a board for Workers' Compensation together, and, since my brother was the Commissioner for Workers' Compensation, they both knew Andy.

"I heard you were coming," Dr. Williams said the first time we met. "You're Andy's sister, and Jane's friend. We'll try to help you all we can while you are here."

He was the largest man I had ever seen walking around like a normal person. I do not mean tall. I mean larger than the Pillsbury Doughboy if he were the size of a person. I instantly decided that he was a heart attack waiting for a place to happen. A few months later

I found out that he ran a weight-loss clinic, somewhere in Lewisburg.

"No way," I told Diamond. "Who would go to a person for weight loss, who has that kind of extreme problem?" We laughed for a long time about the absurdity of that.

Health care was worse than a sick joke.

Things were handled very haphazardly. Procedures and policies were changed without notice. Clinics were run periodically, such as for diabetes and hypertension. However, that doesn't mean that the doctors remembered to write the prescriptions, or, if they were written, that they were given to the pharmacist to be filled.

Once, I waited a week for medication for my blood pressure, and I finally found that my chart had not been given to the pharmacist to fill the prescription. Another woman was given her medication with a wrong name on it.

Dr. Williams was a kind person. He was concerned about my abilities to do certain types of work because my leg was mending and one of the bones in it was still broken.

He was concerned about my blood pressure too, prescribing medication for that, and he wrote work restrictions so that I would not have to do heavy cleaning or be on my feet for any period of time. I do wish that he had diagnosed my physical condition as "fibromyalgia." It was not until a year after I was released that a correct diagnosis was made.

Fibromyalgia is a very painful muscle condition. The causes of it are many, but often it is triggered by an accident. Some have said it is related to arthritis, but the best medication for it is an antidepressant that is a serotonin reuptake suppressor. Once I started taking that type of medication, many of my pain symptoms lessened.

Dr. Williams was an osteopathic physician and would do manipulations of the women's back. Several of them talked about how good the treatment was and how much better they felt after a treatment.

Dr. Shafer was the other physician on staff. He was a gynecologist, and an easy conversationalist. Because his home was in Ohio, I asked why he was working in a West Virginia prison. He said that he liked working with the inmate population, and that he felt he was able to provide a service there that was needed.

Some of the inmates who had been in the prison for a long time had another story to tell. They said that he had been caught in a criminal act and had opted to serve in the prison as a physician instead of going to prison as a convict. Remember that I said that the rumor mill at the prison was fairly accurate, so there is no telling what the truth was. I wondered, *If that rumor is true, then why wasn't I offered something similar?*

There were several physician assistants who provided medical services. Sometimes a doctor would act as a physician's assistant until he or she would be able to obtain a license to practice medicine. That was the case of two of the people on the staff. Both of them were from foreign medical schools and related very well to the Spanish women. Both of them were helpful to me on different occasions. They were good people.

A constant competition existed between the physicians and the physician assistant. They each seemed to have their favorite inmates to take care of, and to provide favors.

The SHRINK

March 8, 1995

Dear Mitch,

Yesterday I had a really nice conversation with Dr. Yale, the psychiatrist. He knows Joe, my doctor, and I gave him written authorization to talk to him. His eyes grew large, showing that he was absolutely flabbergasted that these things have happened to me. He knows that just by the grace of God, or whatever, this, too, could be he. He's prescribing Visteril for sleeping and anxiety. It's an antihistamine, and I can keep it in my room to take it as needed.

Dental Services

It took a long time to get an appointment with the dental clinic. I waited almost a year, but they were very thorough with their work. I liked the woman dentist very much. She was one of the first people I met. She was a part of the Public Health Corp, which is attached to the United States Navy. Many professionals receive money from the government, then repay it by serving in a public health sector, such as a prison or Indian reservation. The first time I met her, I said, "You have really good energy around you." She told me to be careful about people knowing that I was perceptive, because there were many people who didn't understand.

Dental services offered a work training program for dental assistants. It was a year in duration, and competition for acceptance was keen. The women who completed that program had an excellent opportunity for employment when they were released from prison. Some of them received training in a marketable skill that they would probably never have received outside of prison.

"When do you get out of the prison?" the hygienist asked as she did some deep cleaning on my teeth.

"In about six weeks," I answered. "Why?"

"What I see is the beginning of periodontal disease. You should see a periodontist as soon as you can when you are released," she informed me.

I had always prided myself in taking excellent care of my teeth. When I was injured, and when all of the legal problems began, I did not get my teeth cleaned regularly. Now I had a problem. I agreed that I would see a dentist when I returned home.

My dentist did correct the problem very quickly. He praised the dental hygienist for finding my problem while it was still treatable, and so did I.

Eye Care

Eye care was contracted to a female optometrist. She was one of the most sensitive women I have ever met. My eye glasses broke, and I needed a new pair, but the ones I had sent in were not in very good shape, so I made an appointment for an examination and eye glasses.

The day I was there, Marguerite, a new Spanish woman, was there. There was a new rule was that the inmates could not wear contact lenses anymore. Marguerite was crying because she had tremendous problems with eye glasses. Nadine Wilson, the optometrist, had no control over the prison rules. When she was finished with Marguerite, she had tears in her eyes.

"I feel so sorry for these women," she told me, as though I wasn't "one of these women." "I wish I could do more to help them."

"You can," I told her. "Just keep praying us out of here, and that the government isn't so harsh for things that were not done."

Several months after that, I heard a request from her on the Jim Franklin radio ministry program. Prayer was requested that she be able to help the women in prison.

I had the option of two styles of frames for my eye glasses—big and bigger. I chose big. Actually, they were not unlike my other eye glasses that I had worn a few years before. When I went to health services, I saw the bill to the prison for the eye glasses—$17.95. Imagine the markup to the outside world!

Today, I still wear my "prison glasses." Maybe I'll get new ones someday, but I don't need them yet.

Psychobabble

Medical services made referrals to psychological services, and the psychologist was not very personable. I didn't like him from the first time I met him, and I don't think he liked me, either. At one point I was sent to talk to him about the stress I was under. My hair was falling out by handfuls, and he kept me off work for several days, away from the people who were causing the stress. I was positive that he read my report from the Lexington situation and believed everything he read. I often thought about how much good Dr. Wright could have done in Alderson.

At one point, some psychology students were brought in, and I was asked to be interviewed by them. I said, "I will not participate in this unless you force me. I know more than these people do, and I am not going to be their guinea pig." They would have said that I was angry, hostile, and uncooperative, and they would be right. I had no intention of being anything except that with them.

They chose other women. I never questioned the sanity of that decision.

When Tragedy Happens

Lily was a black woman from South Africa. She did not speak English very well, and when she started wailing loudly, it was difficult for anyone to understand what had happened. Finally, Mr. LeRose, the counselor, told us.

Lily had a son who was shot and killed. She was heartbroken, as any mother would have been, whether incarcerated or not. I knew what it felt like to lose a son, because I had a child that died in a fire when he was just past two years old. Lily was given time off from her work assignment.

I went to Lily's room and told her I was sorry. I knew that she wouldn't even remember that had happened, so I wrote a card for her. She could read English, or would have her roommate read to her. I told her that I knew how much it hurt to lose a child, because of my own loss. I wasn't sure Lily knew who I was, but about a week later she came to me.

"You wrote me a card?" Lily asked.

"I did." I acknowledged her with a smile as I put my arm around her shoulder.

"Thank you. It meant more to me than anything else anyone else did, because you told me about your own baby," she said. It was more than I had ever heard Lily speak.

"I am truly sorry for your loss, and if you want to talk I will listen," I offered.

"In Africa we do not speak of the dead," she told me. I already knew that, and told her that I understood that part of her culture.

The card had been acceptable; words of comfort would have been left unacknowledged.

***

Cara Roberts was another black woman who was very young. Just barely twenty-one, she was diagnosed with leukemia upon admittance to the prison.

Cara had blood tests and treatments regularly. "Lynn, I don't know what I would have done if I hadn't been in prison," she told me. "I didn't have any insurance to take care of medical expenses, and I would probably have died." She probably would have died, because the problem would not have been diagnosed. She didn't have any symptoms that would have sent her to the doctor. However, once she was diagnosed, the courts could have released her back to the community, where she could have had treatment. She would have been eligible for Medicaid at that time.

***

Tammy Jamerson's mother died. Tammy was given a furlough to spend time with her before her death. She was very distraught when the call came about her mother. She was given several days off work, but went back to work as soon as possible.

"I'm better off doing something than nothing," she told Lady Di.

***

"Fannie, what's wrong with you?" I asked the woman two doors down the hall from me. She had not been acting right for a couple of days.

We had a good relationship and talked frequently. Sometimes she would do my hair, and sometimes I would share my readings and writings with her.

"Come on and sit," she offered. I knew something was wrong. "Do you know what hepatitis C is?"

"Well, I'm not sure. I do know what hepatitis is, but I don't know much about the classification of it," I admitted. "Why?"

"Do you remember that I have been having blood work done regularly?" she reminded me.

"Yes. What have they found?" I already knew by her previous question.

Somehow Fannie had contracted hepatitis C while she was in the prison system. There is no known cure for hepatitis C, and it will cause the liver to deteriorate and can eventually lead to death.

"Well, what are you going to do about the situation?" I asked. I didn't know what a person could do. There were some administrative remedies, but those would not cure the disease.

Fannie decided to contact a lawyer about the situation, and filed a request for an administrative remedy. The lawyer did not want to be bothered with the case, and the prison said it was not liable for her condition. Fannie still has hepatitis C, and after she was released from prison, she tried working but was not able to continue working. She is receiving social security disability for the deterioration of her liver. Maybe, at some point, she will be eligible for a transplant.

Inmate Illness

It is important not to get sick in prison. One woman thought she was getting the flu, and she was given medicine that made her sicker. Without examining her, they decided that she had the flu, when in actuality she had never eaten cucumbers before, and she had a severe reaction to them. The symptoms were flu-like, with stomach cramps and vomiting, but she also had hives all over her body! Sounded like an allergic reaction to me, but what did I know? I am not a medical doctor.

My Chinese friend, Tina, was having chest pains, and the officer called health services. She had to walk up the hill to health services and was not even examined. She was given an antihistamine. No EKG was administered, and her blood pressure was not taken. She was told to come back the following day. The results were that she suffered from an untreated heart problem.

Another woman was given a pelvic examination and a Pap test. Before the results of the Pap test came back, she was told that she had a yeast infection, and given medication for it. There wasn't any problem, and she didn't take the medication. A month or so later, she was told that she did not have a yeast infection or any other female problems.

A word of warning: Don't get sick in prison. Don't even get the flu. Daisy was sick with the flu, and health services would not write her an "idle" to keep her from working. She worked in food services with the food!

Carlita Santiago was a very dear Spanish-speaking friend. She was twenty-three years old when I met her. She was from Columbia, South America, and had been in prison for several years. Beautiful does not even describe Carlita. As Kathy Patrick, one of the supervisors in food services, said, "She is just such a sweet girl. I can't imagine her doing anything to end up in prison." It was difficult to believe.

"I was visiting here in the States," Carlita related. "I have dual citizenship, but lived with my mother in Columbia. While I was here, I had bad headaches, and went to the doctor. The doctor discovered that I had a brain tumor, and I needed surgery. The medical bills were going to cost more than $45,000. I didn't have any money. Some people I knew told me that they would give me that much money if I would pass some drugs to some people. I agreed to do it, and was arrested for selling drugs. When I was taken in front of the judge, he asked me why I did what I did, and I told him about the brain tumor." She smiled when she told me this. "Now, what judge would ever begin to believe such a story?

"Well, he said that he would check out my records and try to decide what to do if I was telling the truth. He discovered that I was telling the truth and arranged to have the surgery performed. I am in prison, but I would have been dead if the surgery had not been done."

The surgery left Carlita with seizures, but the medication controlled them. She was carefully checked medically for any problems. She was glad to be in the prison at Alderson and not in a medical facility somewhere. "I don't hate it here," she told me. "I wish there had been some other way for me to be healed, but most of the people are good to me here." Carlita took medicine every day, and I wondered how she would manage when she was released, because the medications that she took were very expensive, and I wondered how she would afford them.

"Where's Donna?" I asked Lady Di.

"Oh, didn't you hear?" Diane answered. "They found her in a diabetic coma last night and took her to the hospital in Lewisburg."

Donna knew better than to not take her medicine. She had been diabetic for a long time, and since she was a veterinarian, she knew and understood medicine. This was not the first time this happened to Donna.

"Lt. Stone, what happened to Donna?" we asked one of the staff.

"The doctors are transferring her to Carswell, because she needs intensive medical management, and she won't comply with treatment here," Lt. Stone informed us. "She will be moved in a day or two. She is doing all right, though."

Lady Di and I talked about her. How could this well-educated woman be so stupid? Her insulin needed to be monitored three times a day, and she would try taking less insulin because she thought she was going to be healed.

I tried talking sense into her one day before this incident. "Donna, your diabetes is controlled, and control is as good as healed."

"No, it isn't, " she insisted.

"You're going to wake up dead some morning," I warned her.

I sent her a Christmas card after we were both released from the prison. The card was returned to me marked: Deceased. Return to Sender.

Donna had died, just as I predicted.

Chapter 7

Hi, Ho! To Work We Go

Get a Job

Glasses, forks, and knives, and spoons. Glasses, forks, and knives, and spoons, I sang to myself to the tune of the little children's song, "Head, shoulders, knees and toes."

"Get a job" is the first thing I was told. Getting a job actually meant finding a place for the woman to be during the day time. Some of the jobs, such as landscape and ground maintenance, were actual work, while other jobs consisted of sitting most of the day, doing very little of anything else.

Finding a job seemed to be more a matter of whom one knew, rather than what kind of skills the woman had or what she could do to best serve the institution. The rule was to leave your brain at the gate, so if what you wanted to do made any sense, it would be denied. What was wanted by the staff seemed to be sheer, brute labor, not intelligence.

The women worked as library aides, clerks, secretaries, receptionists, maintenance workers, landscape workers, plumbers, masons, electricians, boiler room laborers, cooks, waitresses, dish room operators, warehouse laborers, teacher aides, drivers, and chapel aides.

I had always worked, and I never had difficulty finding or being hired for a job until I went to prison. I knew that I was unable to do manual work because I was not able to be on my leg very long and, if I were, I'd be in pain. Perhaps it was selfish or self-centered, but I did not want to work as a "teacher's aide," especially after my experience with the staff in the educational facility. My preference was the chapel or the library, but the chapel was a clique which was impossible to break into at that time, and the library didn't have any openings. For four months I worked in food service before I found another position.

The one thing that I liked about food service was that I didn't have to be there until 10:30 in the morning, because I have never been a person who liked to get up early. The other thing that I liked was that there were not as many people in the dining room when we ate because we had earlier meals than the rest of the women.

Later, I was to find out that West Virginia's former governor, Arch Moore, who was sentenced to prison for bribery and extortion, worked in food services in the men's prison in Huntsville, Alabama, managing the salad bar.

What I didn't like was the management in food services. I have an undergraduate degree in home economics and, had I taken one more class, I could have managed a facility such as the prison food services. The man who was the manager had a college education, but he had no people skills and did nothing to resolve problems. The correctional officers, who were food staff foremen, were either liked or disliked by the women. Those who were disliked had no people skills, and those who were liked did.

Ms. Jackson and Ms. Patrick had excellent rapport with the women. Ms. Arthur did with some women, but not all. Everything depended on her mood. The day one of the women threw food all over me was a day when she was very good to me. Her behavior was dependent on her emotions.

Male foremen had their own set of problems. Mr. George was nice, but he would flirt with the women, and then they thought that he was favoring them. Mr. Thornton's temperament changed frequently, but was much more even tempered than Ms. Arthur. He was fair, whereas Ms. Arthur wasn't.

Mr. Whitehall had a kind heart. He was also a preacher, and would come back to the prison and preach in the chapel at night. He was short, and when he started preaching, his voice rose higher than he was tall. Frequently, we would sit and talk about spiritual truths, and how God speaks to each of us in different ways. I liked the food that was prepared in food service when Mr. Whitehall was in charge of the kitchen, and I told him so. He had learned to cook while he was in the military. After leaving the military, he took a job as a correctional officer, where he then moved into food service. When he preached in the chapel in the evenings, sometimes I would go to the services and play the piano for him. If I didn't, no one else volunteered to play. He always allowed the women to leave work early to attend church services on Sunday.

The biggest problem that the staff had in food services was "Buffalo Bob." He was a problem to the prison and was moved from one job to another. He was a correctional officer, then worked in the factory, and then he moved to food services. What skills gave him that position is something that no one could ever understand. It's important to remember that a prison is just like any other business. It is difficult to fire a person without a large amount of documentation for misconduct.

The correctional officers had a union, and Ms. Jackson was the union president. She had a legal problem with the prison several years before, when she became convinced of the need for a union. Other officers frequently came into the food service building to talk with her about the union. At times, she and the other union officers would meet in the staff dining room, to discuss various problems.

The problems in food service revolved around competition and jealousy among the staff, favoritism to various women, and blatant incompetency. Some of the work was physically difficult for me, especially mopping floors. Each woman working in the dining room would be assigned to sweep and mop part of the floor. It really didn't take very long, but when I would be finished, I was almost unable to walk.

My goal was to find some other place to be. Basically, finding a job was a place to be during the day. I needed to be somewhere else.

A New Job

Something had to change. Working in the factory which produced items for the government was like working for slave wages. I was not going to prostitute my sewing talents by working for the government. My education would have allowed me to manage the sewing factory, too.

Finally, I was accepted at the power house. The prison used to generate its own electricity, but now only generated steam power. The tasks at the power house were simple. Meters had to be read every hour, on the hour. Floors had to be mopped before evening; equipment had to be cleaned. Most of the rest of the time the women could write, read, talk, study, or do whatever they wanted. All the men who worked there, with the exception of one, did not press the women to do very much.

Haggy, the power house shift supervisor, went to a cabinet next to where I was sitting, to inventory some paint for the painters. " Well, f--k." He looked at me with an "oh-my-gosh-what-did-I-say" look and said, "Oh, ma'am. I'm sorry."

I laughed because he'd called me ma'am, and thought I hadn't heard that "word" used before! People always looked at me as though I were innocent. "Nothing to apologize for," I told him. "The word is merely an acronym that means 'fornication and unlawful carnal knowledge.' It was derived during the time of the pilgrims, when they put people in stocks for having sex out of marriage."

"Say that again," he said. I repeated what I had just told him.

"Hey, George! Come here!" Haggy called the plumber.

George came at a fast clip."What's wrong? What's wrong?"

"Tell George what you just said." Haggy's mischievous look told me that he was up to something.

I repeated what I had told Haggy.

"Well, I'll be damned," George laughed. "Now, tell me that again so I won't forget it." I repeated my four-letter word story again. It wasn't long before my story was told to all of the men working in the trades and skills.

I liked being there, and I liked most of the men. It was my belief that many men who work in the trades and skills were above average in intelligence. Most of the men were bright and interesting to talk to because their job was not their only interest. Two of the men really enjoyed history and shared my books with me.

It seemed that they enjoyed working with me. I was given bonuses, which I never received in food services, and excellent reports by everyone except one man. I was later to understand that he was another one of the prison employee "problems."

For three months I worked in the power house. The work was interesting. I had to find out how everything worked and what did what. I didn't even mind wearing steel-toed shoes while I was there. Much of the time I was able to write, which I did. I even discovered that I could mop the floor without tiring my back. There was nothing in the way, just open floor space, so I could pull the mop around behind me.

Then, one day, I was arbitrarily transferred back to food services. One of the men who worked there went through the list of women who had work restrictions, and they were all transferred. My only restriction was "no ladders or climbing."

I was hysterical. It was unfathomable that my seniority could be stripped from me because one man, Jack Peters, had taken a dislike to me. Hysterical wasn't the word for it. I knew that if I didn't get some medicine, I would be ill. Roger Combs was working, and called the staff in my cottage so that I could talk to them.

"Lynn, the food service people asked for you by name," Mr. Hendricks told me.

"Get off it," I told him. "That's not the way it happened. Jack Peters didn't want me there, and he had the authority to make the selection as to who went and who stayed. That is not fair!" My body shook as though I was in shock. It was uncontrollable.

"We can't change this," Mr. LaRose said. "It's the same kind of thing they have done to us at times." He was referring to being a prison employee.

"Do you want to go to health services?" Mr. Hendricks asked.

"I guess I'll have to. I'll have to have restrictions because I am not mopping floors with all these younger, healthier women around." I was still shaking and hysterical. "Prison is supposed to be punishment. But those people in food services think that they are part of the process." I knew my face was red and my eyes swollen.

There was no problem getting the sweeping and mopping restrictions from health services. I filed a grievance against the prison for inappropriately transferring me back to food services. I even contacted the law students who came to the prison every month from Washington and Lee University. Nothing helped. In my heart I knew that it was all part of the government. One person upheld another. Nothing would ever be resolved.

Some of the staff members in food services were angry that I had the restrictions from health services.

"Why didn't you get these restrictions when you were in here before?" one of them asked me.

"I thought I could endure anything for two months, but I hurt so badly that I was unable to do anything except get in bed. I have a right to live, even while I am here," I answered.

Ms. Patrick and Ms. Jackson were glad I was back. Ms. Patrick was having as much trouble dealing with the rest of the staff as I was. "Do you think I'll make it here?" Kathy asked me frequently. She was assertive, but she was up against treachery. After I was released, I found out that she stopped working in food services and returned to her previous position as a correctional officer.

I couldn't count the number of people I talked with about transferring to another job. I was promised this and that by various staff, but there was always some excuse as to why that wasn't available.

The prison had three people who were major employee problems, and I had run-ins with all three of them. It was obvious that Dickerson and "Buffalo Bob" drank off the job. I wondered if they drank on the job, too, but I never saw any indication that would prove that they did.

"Buffalo Bob" had a terrible disposition. He would be nice, and then obnoxious. He liked the morning workers much better than the afternoon workers and, almost without exception, allowed them to leave before their work was finished.

One day a woman left mop, pail and water in the middle of the floor. She was lazy and never did her share of work. I was really irritated.

"Why did you let her leave?" I asked "Buffalo Bob." "She didn't finish the floor."

"You can finish it," he told me.

"I do not do floors because I have restrictions, and I have no intention of causing myself pain by mopping floors when there was someone else to do it, and you let her go." I was not rude or nasty.

"It wouldn't hurt you to do it," he told me, not looking at me when he spoke.

I immediately got up, went to the assistant food service manager, Mr.Epling, and told him about the situation.

A little later "Buffalo Bob" came out to where I was sitting.

"Ms. Hartz," he started, "if there is anything I hate, it is a snitch. If you expect to not have any trouble while you are here, I suggest that you keep your mouth shut, and we'll get along just fine."

He had another thing coming, if he thought he was going to intimidate me. "Then honor the restrictions."

He just threatened me, I thought.

The following day I told Captain Shumaker what had happened. "I felt as though it were a threat," I told him.

"As soon as you're finished here, go see Lieutenant Wolf," he instructed me. "I want him to take a statement from you."

An hour later I was telling Lieutenant Wolf the story. "It won't do any good for me to tell you this and sign a statement that it happened. You all will never do anything to resolve the problems of the troublemakers on staff here." He knew that I was disgusted with "Buffalo Bob."

"We can't do anything without documentation to back up whatever happens," he told me. I answered his questions and signed a statement. Wondering if anything could be done about him or anyone else who abused their authority and power, I doubted that there would ever be any resolution to the situation.

My own solution came when I realized that I could take days off for vacation time. I scheduled my vacation days to coincide with the days that "Buffalo Bob" was the supervisor, and then I could avoid that stress.

Conflict avoidance is one way of managing. It was easier than any more confrontation.

The Blizzard and the Flood

The prison was subject to weather problems the same as any other place. In January it started snowing. It snowed and it snowed and it snowed some more. The deeper it became, the more indescribably beautiful and incredibly dangerous it became. Soon, the snow was as deep as my waist. I felt terror at the thought of trying to walk from one place to another in the deep snow. It was a blizzard like I never experienced before, and I lived in West Virginia most of my life. All of Southern West Virginia was hit harder than any other place around.

Grounds maintenance worked night and day plowing the snow. The women who worked on the equipment worked long, cold hours. I felt sorry for them.

During the day light hours it wasn't too difficult to get around. But in January darkness falls about five o'clock in the mountains, and it gets cold very quickly. That meant that whatever had melted from being walked upon would be frozen and treacherous.

Diamond and I walked to food services together, but she finished her work early and left. When I finished, I could either walk around the long way, or try a short cut where the snow was about three feet deep and had not been plowed. I opted for the latter. Wrong choice!

I fell and didn't think I was going to be able to get back up. My heart started pounding, and I felt anxiety spread quickly over my total being. There was no one else around to help me up. It had been a long time since I felt so totally alone and frightened.

Dear God, please give me the strength to get up out of here, I prayed in my mind.

I do not know how I got up. When I did, I was covered with snow and freezing slush.

"Did you fall?" Diamond asked when she saw my wet clothes.

"Sure did," I told her. "Don't tell anyone, though. I don't want to be teased. I really felt fear and panic while getting back on my feet." I changed my clothes and sat in a hot tub until I felt thawed. Those old-fashioned, claw-footed bathtubs were deep and the soak felt good. I knew that it kept me from being sore from falling. I hoped that I wouldn't fall again, because when the snow would melt, the water would freeze at night, causing more hazardous conditions.

The snow took weeks to melt. As it began to melt, the town of Alderson, as well as all of Southern West Virginia, started flooding. The Greenbrier River overflowed its banks. From one side of the food services building I could sit and watch people's possessions overtaken by rushing river. I saw portable buildings swept away and mobile homes carried away by the water. Even a satellite dish went floating down the river. I wondered what was happening the other side of the river because some of the people were unable to cross the bridge to get to the prison. It was a mess.

The greatest problem that the prison experienced was a water problem. There was not a problem with water standing on the ground, the problem was with the water that was for drinking and utilitarian purposes. The water came from the town of Alderson, and that water was contaminated. Pipes bringing the water into the prison broke, and it was several weeks before they were fixed.

I wrote to Fred and Macy on January 22:

> *The water is off all over the prison campus except in food service. Water has to be carried to the cottages, and it is a big mess. The toilets can't be flushed, and no one can shower or bathe. There is one thing I know, however: there isn't anything wrong with the water! If there were a problem, the water in food service would be bad and could not be used.*

The problem is the sewer system. If it filled up, it would back up and be a really serious health problem. I can't figure out why they lie to us about the situation.

A gallon of drinking water a day was given to each woman. The National Guard brought water in. Showers were nonexistent for a few days, but then five-minute showers were allotted. An officer sat outside the shower room and timed the women, then would call for the next person. Some of the women tried to take advantage of the opportunity to shower and took too much time. Food service workers were allowed to shower daily.

The women inmates were asked to go out into the community of Alderson and help clean up. Many volunteered and said they felt a great sense of accomplishment for their work. *The Charleston Gazette* carried a front page article about the women helping the town. I did not volunteer to help because I knew that I was not able to do what needed to be done.

The Fire Department

It would be unfair to write about any prison experiences in Alderson and leave the most important feature of the prison out.

Alderson Federal Women's Prison Camp has the only all-female fire department in the world. Women volunteer to be on the fire department, and they live in a special cottage. The women are trained and certified as firefighters through the West Virginia State Fire Marshall's office.

The women are issued uniforms and have their own jackets with their names on them. It is a privilege to be chosen as a firefighter.

The women firefighters worked in conjunction with the Alderson Volunteer Fire Department and had the opportunity to go outside the prison to back up the Town of Alderson Fire Department when necessary. They also participated in the town parades.

During the blizzard and resulting flood, the firefighters worked night and day hauling water, flushing the toilets in all the cottages with the water that was brought into the prison, working outside the prison, and helping the National Guard in any way that was needed.

I knew a few of the women who were firefighters fairly well. Jean Camarato had not been in the prison for very long, and she was only twenty-three years old. She was a pretty, dark-eyed woman with curly black hair. She worked in food services handing clerical work for the officers.

One day Jean sat next to me. "Lynn, I'm worried about taking the fire department test," she told me.

"Why?" I questioned her. "You're a smart girl. You'll do fine."

"Oh, I guess I'm just scared. I want it so much. I think I would like to be a professional when I am released."

"If you need reassurance from me, you've got it," I told her. "If you are asking me if you'll pass the test, the answer is 'yes.' You will miss a couple of questions that will make you feel irritated when you realize how you answered them, but you will get your certification."

My pretty young friend touched my hand. "Thanks, Lynn!"

A few weeks later she told me that she had passed. She had missed a couple of questions that she thought she should have known.

There were two other women on the fire department that I really liked. Crystal Mays was a tall, slender woman, with a slight tinge of red to her light brown hair. Her job was working in the recreation department. I liked her because she was very open-minded, and she had a deep sense of her own spirituality. Crystal enjoyed the fire department.

"I work hard when we have to go on a call," she told me. "It's worth it, though, because I feel so worthwhile, and I know I am doing something good." Crystal was in prison for drug conspiracy, but she was not a user. She was involved with a man who used and sold drugs. So many of the women were in prison because of something that a man involved them in.

Mari Miller was another woman on the fire department. She was a dental hygienist and worked in the dental office. Mari was a little person with dark hair, very light skin, and brown eyes. It was not easy to picture this demure woman in prison, much less on the fire department.

"I might be small, but I'm healthy," she told me. Whatever she did to be sentenced to prison was something to do with a money problem through the place where she worked. She was from Ohio, and her parents came to visit her at least once a month.

These were the women who helped keep the prison safe. They helped keep the town of Alderson safe, too. They deserved all of the good wishes and accolades that were bestowed upon them. Their training was invaluable.

Chapter 8

Fun and Leisure Time

Playtime

People who are incarcerated will find a way to play and have recreation, regardless of the circumstances. This is true for long-term rehabilitation, such as the old tuberculosis hospitals and other types of rehabilitation facilities. Many of the women crocheted and knitted. Their work was outstanding.

"If I buy the yarn, will you make my daughters three of those dolls?" I asked Helen Trump.

"Sure." She was glad. She knew that I would also pay her a little or pick up some items at the commissary for her.

They were cute little crocheted guys that could sit on a shelf or a bed. All but one was finished before Christmas. I had wondered how I would be able to do something special for my daughters for Christmas. Usually, I made them something, but I did not have my own sewing machine, and trying to use what was in the prison was impossible. Besides, having material sent in was expensive because it had to be purchased through the recreation department, and it was a lot of trouble. But they had dolls—one green, one purple, and one multicolored.

At another time my Chinese friend, Tina, asked me if she could knit me a vest. I was delighted! She knitted a red pullover vest, and I added a fringe to it. I wasn't sure why I was treated with such a wonderful gift of time and love, but I was learning to be on the receiving end of goodness and love.

***

"Miss Diamond, can I speak to you out in the hall?" Terri Parks, one of the attractive, young black women, came to our room and asked for my roommate. Terri was only twenty-three years old, and in prison for drug conspiracy. I had no idea what Terri wanted with Diamond, but I could hear through the door.

"Yes. No, I don't mind. How much do you want?" It had to be money because my roommate was known to have money whenever she wanted it.

"What was that all about?" I asked Diamond when she came back.

"Terri wants to play cards, and she can't get any money out of the commissary until next week," she stated.

"Oh. Okay. So, you're the bank." I laughed. I liked Terri. She always called me "Miss Lynn." She didn't have to do that, but she said, "Miss Lynn, that is how my Mama taught me. We were taught to be respectful to women older than us, and that is how we show our respect." Terri always paid her debts back, and she didn't usually lose any money.

Those cold winter nights were usually filled with women playing Spades. I had never heard of Spades, but found out it was played like the card game Hearts, which was my favorite card game.

Money in the prison was a little odd. There were no dollar bills or pennies, just nickels, dimes and quarters—mostly quarters. Diamond and I usually had plenty of quarters, and most people knew who had a little money.

If Diamond ran out, I was next on the list. I didn't mind lending the women a little money, or even getting a candy bar or a bottle of soda occasionally. It was returned to me in so many ways.

Not only did the women know who had a little money, they also knew who had extra food if a party was planned, or who had stamps.

I never had anyone steal anything from me, except the first roommate I had. She stole my money, my towels that had been sent in to me, and my picture coupons.

It was Jackie Romero's second time in prison. She had violated her probation, or halfway house, gotten pregnant, and was sent back to prison. She said that the baby was her husband's, but there were plenty of doubts about that. This was my first daily encounter with a true sociopath. The day that she left, my towels were missing, and so were my photo coupons. Jackie even had the audacity to brag to me that she had a friend who had given her photo coupons, and she and her friends were going to have their pictures made.

In a letter I wrote I said:

> *I'm singing a new song. "Thank God and Greyhound She's Gone!" My roommate left Sunday. She was a complete psychopath. She took things from everyone. I think she was a kleptomaniac. Jackie left here with one girl's shirt and shoes, another one's socks, and my towels. She stole money, stamps, food and picture coupons from me. She lied about where she was going. She said she was going home, but I saw her travel papers, and she had to go to a halfway house. So right now I'm without a roommate.*

As soon as I realized what had happened, I reported it to the officer on duty. We tried to get my photo coupons back, but it was too late. I just didn't speak to her again, since she was leaving the next morning. A good riddance. I was sure that she would be back in prison.

***

"Lynn, come walk with us," Lady Di said, as she and Jeannie Rogers and a couple of other women from food services decided to take an afternoon break.

"I don't think I can handle it," I replied, knowing that I was limited in my ability to walk for any distance. They walked every day. Some of the women walked every evening, listening to their radios or tape players or walking with a companion.

"I feel so free here," Sherry told me once when she stopped to talk to me while she was walking. "I lived in the middle of Philadelphia, and you couldn't walk anywhere, any place, especially at night. I love the nights here." And Sherry was right. You could walk anywhere safely. The more women I knew, the more I was learning about the lives the women endured before coming to prison. My life was drastically different.

The recreation department offered aerobic exercise classes every evening, usually three or four classes each evening. Many of the women participated in these, or led the classes.

Write, Write, Write

Lynn, you're the only person I know that could make being incarcerated in a women's prison sound like going to a writer's colony, my friend, Bunny, wrote me from California. She was one of my oldest and dearest friends from high school. I had written to her about my life and my writing.The day I entered the prison I started writing. As long as I had a mind, I would not go crazy, because I could think of things to write. I first started on a novel that I called *And Time Stood Still*. Finding enough paper to write on was a problem because the officers were stingy with giving out paper. When I had my box of personal items sent in, I had notebooks included.

The novel was about the midwife who delivered the Christ Child. I had read a little about a midwife in the Apocryphal Gospel of Mary and thought it would be a fascinating story to develop. I wrote until my fingers hurt. In June, five months after I had started writing, I wrote to my Uncle Fred and Aunt Macy:

> *I finished the first draft of the book I was writing about the midwife that delivered the Christ Child . . . I have some errors in the story line, mostly of a historical nature, and I want to add some things to it. I have written over 200 pages of it by hand. Would you believe my hands hurt? My fingers have calluses on them and are very sore from holding a pen. I*

wonder if you can get carpal tunnel syndrome from writing?

How I wished I had a typewriter!

There were typewriters available in the library, but you had to buy your own ribbon. The library wasn't open all the time, however, and other people wanted to use the typewriters, too.

So I continued writing by hand. "Sharon," I said to my sister-in-law on the telephone, "if I send you my hand written manuscript, will you type it for me, then send it back into me?"

"I'd be glad to do that," she graciously agreed. Sharon, Andy's wife, also liked to write, and she had several articles published. She knew that this would help me. I hated to let go of the manuscript as I put what I had in the mail to her.

Once my original was mailed, I could not refer to something that I had already written. This proved to be a problem in sequencing my storyline.

Well, I thought. *I might as well start on something else while I wait*. That is when I developed the idea for writing about prison life. I wrote little things and sent them out to my other sister-in-law, Jamie. If I had access to it, I could have kept a complete secretarial staff on the outside busy. Sharon and Jamie both had many other things to do, so I didn't get my work back very quickly.

One day Sharon and I were talking on the telephone. "Lynn, I was walking with my neighbor and was telling her about Lydia (the name I gave the midwife). She said that she didn't know that there was a midwife named Lydia! I told her that there is now!"

Several other women were writing, too. We should have had a writer's group. I guess we just never thought about doing that. One woman was writing about her experiences in the federal prison. She called hers, *Unforgiven and Forgotten*. I thought her work should do well. She had a friend who was trying to get her work on the Internet, and I didn't think that was the best way to go.

Another woman was writing romance novels. She used an American Indian theme, because she had Indian heritage. She worked diligently on her ideas.

My friend, Donna Hawthorne, consistently worked on a book, too. Her writing themes were mystical, metaphysical, and very deeply spiritual. Donna had experienced severe depression, which led her to the commission of a money crime. Now, she was recovering from both the crime and the depression. I liked Donna, and greatly admired her perseverance.

One day I was teasing one of the male officers. He was sitting in the office of the cottage and was talking about the amount of mail Diamond and I received—again. I told him when I write my book I was going to identify him as "Houston." His look said, "Yeah, right." I also told him that I would identify him as one of the "good guys," and asked him where his "white hat" was. (Remember in the cowboy movies that the good guys always wear the white hats?)

"How are you going to identify Baxter?" Houston asked. Baxter was sitting there talking.

"Oh, I probably won't even mention him," I laughed. "He doesn't ever talk to me and he always reads my newspaper, and doesn't even say 'thanks.' " Baxter just looked at me with his usual deadpan expression. He wasn't mean or nasty; he was just "there."

As I was sitting with some women in food service one day, I was telling them about a new idea.

"I think I'll write a book that will be fictionalized fact," I said.

"What in the heck is that?" Opal Chapman asked. Opal was a black woman about my age who had tried smuggling drugs in to her son, who was in prison. Guess what happened to Opal? You know where I met her.

"It will be fiction, but the characters will be developed from real people that I know, or that other people know and tell me about," I explained. "I thought I would develop a person who would be a combination of my father and my grandfathers," I continued. "All of these men were very interesting, and I thought a combination character would put their traits together, and I could develop a novel from it."

"That makes sense. It sounds like fun, too," Lady Di said. We were taking a break, sharing some of the extra desserts and drinking sodas.

A few days later I had developed the idea a little further. "Come on, you all. Sit here and help me develop some character names and ideas." Opal, Lady Di and Jennifer sat down. A few minutes later two other women, Dottie Jefferson and Miss Hawaii, joined us.

"Now, this is a rather complex story," I told them. "The man's name is John Anderson and he is an ordinary man who lives an ordinary life, but to his family and friends he is a hero. He has a wife, Edith, and four children, two girls and two boys. In the first chapter he dies, and in the last chapter he is buried. All the chapters in between will tell the story of his life."

"Well, what are the names of the children?" Lady Di asked. That was all I had. I had the four children, but no names for his brothers and sisters, grandchildren, or aunts and uncles, and cousins.

"I think it is going to get so complicated that I'll need to draw a family tree," I said, getting out a large piece of paper.

The group soon had a complete family tree, with names for everyone. The names and relationships that we developed as I worked on that novel are what I used in the book.

I started another nonfiction work about people in prison. Researching the Bible and identifying biblical characters who were imprisoned was time consuming. I decided to include Jonah, who, although he was not in a prison, most surely was in the belly of a fish.

For a short time while I was working in the power house, Tanya Rogers, one of the women who also worked there, wanted to read my work.

"I'm working on Jonah right now," I told her. "I'm almost finished, then I'm going to do Daniel."

Tanya was in prison as an accessory to interstate gun selling. She said that she and her husband had licenses to deal in guns, and that they never dealt in stolen merchandise, but she believed that they were accused of crimes because they were black people operating a business usually handled by white people. "Oh, Lynn!" Tanya said as she began to read. "I am beginning to understand what has happened to me!"

"What do you mean?" I needed to know what had touched her.

"I thought that God forgot about me, and I couldn't make any sense about any of this, but, Jonah couldn't either. He finally developed some understanding, though, and now I do understand."

A couple of weeks later Tanya was called to her case manager's office. Her case had been reviewed, and she was given an immediate release. She walked down to the power house to tell us goodbye.

"I'm going to miss you," I told her. "I have truly enjoyed knowing you, and I am delighted you're going home."

"I'll never forget you, not ever!" Tanya hugged me back. I knew that she had touched my heart and soul, and I would never forget her. What I thought had been so little, seemed to her to be so much. My writing had instilled hope in her. Hope is the total, essential quality for surviving any negative experience.

The concept of this book expanded in my mind. I began calling it *Praise Him in Prison*. I had finished all of the Biblical people, then decided to expand the idea. The first part, I identified as "Biblical Characters Praise Him in Prison." I identified the second part as, "Other People Praise Him in Prison." I decided to include people like Charles Colson, St. Patrick, Joan of Arc and Dietrich Bonhoeffer.

"Ms. Haynes, I need some books that aren't in the library here," I told the woman who ran the library services. She and I liked each other, and I knew that she would help in whatever way she could.

"Well, what are you working on now?" Ms. Haynes asked. I frequently shared my ideas with her. I developed and provided a couple of afternoon workshops for the women, one on "Metaphysics" and another on "Dreams and Dream Interpretation." The attendance at both was excellent. I was asked to provide some more, but it wasn't always possible because the day would interfere with my visits.

"I am expanding my ideas about people in prison and how they use God to cope," I told her. "This is my list so far. There are a few things here, but there are some that I can't find. I would like something on St. Patrick and Dietrich Bonhoeffer. The encyclopedias don't have enough."

"This might take some research." She smiled. I knew that she would find whatever she could.

A couple of weeks later one of the women who worked in the library saw me in food services. "Your book is in," she told me. I could hardly wait to get to the library to see what was there.

Letters from Prison by Dietrich Bonhoeffer! Tears welled up in my eyes because I was so delighted. Then, when I saw where it came from, I was thrilled.

West Virginia has a wonderful library system, as part of the Culture and Archives Division. It was conceived and developed by Fred Glazer, and had received many national awards. It was possible to identify where every book in every library in the State of West Virginia is at any given time. Ms. Haynes found the Bonhoeffer book at the library in the Cultural Center. They then sent it to the prison, on loan for two weeks.

Usually, books that were sent on a loan were not allowed out of the library, but Ms. Haynes allowed me to keep it in my room for the duration of the loan. I read it, and then made copies of various pages to use for quotations.

I felt the spirit of God touch me as I read about Dietrich Bonhoeffer. He was a part of the German resistance. When the Allies went in to liberate Germany, the German soldiers hung Bonhoeffer the day before the Allies arrived. I knew that God had used him during his prison time, but I was unable to understand why God didn't intervene before the hanging.

Someday I was sure that I would find answers to my questions. I started another outline for a future book that I titled, *The Answer to, Why Me?* It was a beginning.

I've mentioned before the number of letters that I wrote. In one letter to my Uncle Fred and Aunt Macy I told them that I had hand written 33 pages that day.

> *Just call this place "Club Fed" . . . You know what possession I miss the most? My word processor. I write by hand so much that I have calluses on my fingers!*

I wrote again later:

I write so much that I have to keep my nails trimmed, and periodically I have to stop and heal the calluses on my fingers . . .

Visits

The first weekend I was in the prison, I had a visit. I was so surprised. My sister, Jean, and her new husband came. They called and talked to a staff person who gave them permission to come. That was the first of many visits that Jean and her husband made to see me.

During the early part of my stay, Jean became sick and was hospitalized for depression. She started having panic attacks, and soon was totally unable to work. She had trouble driving and came to see me only if her husband would bring her. One day, after I had talked with her on the telephone, she attempted driving by herself. It was a Monday, and she arrived, depressed and panicky, but she made it. That day, I felt as though my whole purpose for being was to counsel her through some of the problems that she was experiencing. I worried about her driving home, so I called her later in the evening to make sure she was home safely. She was.

My brother, Ray, married Jamie Sullivan on March 24, 1995, which was a Saturday, and they came to visit me the next day.

"You came to the prison for your honeymoon!" I teased as soon as I saw them.

"I didn't even think of that!" Jamie hugged me. "I just knew that we missed you and wanted to see you."

We had a wonderful visit. The next day I told the warden, Mr. Wils, that my brother got married, and he and his new wife came to the prison to visit me for their honeymoon.

He laughed. "I don't think my sister cares that much for me," he said. I knew that he would appreciate the humor.

That is only one example of the support that I received from my family and friends. Not everyone had that kind of love and support.

***

"My sweetheart is coming to visit today," I told Kathy Patrick, one of the supervisors in the kitchen.

She looked at me with her snappy eyes. "What else is new? Is there any time that he doesn't come to see you?" She grinned as we sat and chatted over beverages on a Saturday morning. We had a "mutual admiration society." She was a tiny, short woman, and I wondered how she met the requirements to be hired by the BOP. Kathy was only about four feet, nine inches tall.

"He's really good to me," I told her. "I think I must be the luckiest gal in the world to have him."

"I know how you feel," she responded. "My husband's like that, too. What time's he going to be here?"

"Well, about now, if he arrives about the same time as he usually does," I answered. Mitch was always on time or early. One thing I liked about him was that he was seldom ever late, and if he was, there was something wrong, such as bad traffic or an accident somewhere.

Just then the telephone rang, and Kathy went to answer it. I knew it was the visiting room calling to tell me Mitch was there.

I got up to leave as Kathy answered the phone. She turned around and looked at me and waved as she said, "Have a good time, and I'll see you tomorrow!"

I knew it was Mitch, but what I didn't know was that he brought our good friend, Ray Landers, with him. I walked into the visiting room, and Mitch was in his usual place, but he looked like the cat that just ate the mouse.

"What's up?" I asked, and then I saw Ray. I ran and gave him as hug.

"Oh, Ray! I'm so glad to see you!" I exclaimed as I almost knocked him over with my exuberance.

Ray came to visit me with Mitch several times. He brought pictures for me to see of him with his children on horses at a friend's farm. He told me about his friend, Mike Craigo, a "horse whisperer." I was to meet Mike at Ray's son Josh's wedding after I was released from prison.

Ray's wife and I were friends, too, but Patsy could not bring herself to come to the prison to visit me. I understood how she felt, but I missed her. She and Ray were the first people to visit me when I arrived home. "You're back where you belong," she told me. "I couldn't bear to see you there, but I didn't forget you for a day, and I prayed for you every day." I knew she had.

One of the days that Ray came with Mitch to visit, another man was visiting his sister.

"Look at that man with the two different shoes on," Ray noticed. "Doesn't that look silly? Why would someone do that?"

I hadn't paid any attention. I was more curious about who had the limousine bring them to the prison to visit.

The man with the different shoes was pleasant and friendly. *Just odd*, I thought. It was a while later before I figured out who he was. Tom Arnold was visiting his sister, Lori.

I had a visit almost every weekend. My dear, beloved Mitch came almost every weekend. One weekend in August he didn't come.

"Lt. Stone, I got stood up by a cow! Mitch went out and bought a heifer instead of coming to see me!" I told Lt. Stone, one of the officers that I liked. She knew Mitch from meeting him in the visiting room, and I knew about her farm. She and her husband raised cattle.

"Well, Lynn, I'll bet that cow will bring in more money than you will while you're here!" she laughed. I told several other people and they thought it was funny, too. Stood up by a cow!

***

"You have a visit," announced the officer, coming to my room.

"I do?" I looked at her quizzically. "I'm not expecting anyone."

"Well, someone's here to surprise you." She was friendly, and I liked this gal.

I changed my clothes and went to the visiting room. I had a feeling that I knew who it was. I was so pleased. My next-door neighbors from home had come to visit, and brought their little girl!

Bill and Pam Arthur and their daughter Ashley were wonderful neighbors. They had only lived in the house next to mine for about three years. They were both lawyers, but Pam stayed at home with their daughter.

"Pam! Bill! I knew it was you! Hi, Ash." I greeted them all with hugs. "Let's take Ash outside where she can play," I suggested.

"We've been down to Camp Wimpy," Pam explained. Camp Wimpy belonged to her parents, and it was located in Greenbrier County not very far from the prison.

I laughed. "I'll bet you're tired of camping," I teased.

"Yeah," Bill said. "Pam's dad thinks it's fun, but it's a lot of work with a baby. Come, Ash. Let's put you in a swing while your mother talks with Lynn." Ashley looked exactly like her father. She attached herself to him like a baby monkey.

Pam and I sat down to talk. "I'm sorry I haven't written for a while," she began to apologize.

"You don't have to apologize, Pam," I told her. "You have a life and a baby. . ."

"Well, let me explain. Ashley got the chicken pox, then I got the chicken pox and we've been really, really sick." She showed me some pock marks.

"Oh, gosh, Pam. That's dangerous for adults. Are you okay, now?"

"I feel all right, but we've been trying to get pregnant again, and the doctor is concerned that the chicken pox might have created a problem," she confided.

"I guess we'd better pray about that, then," I told her. "Have fun trying, and one of these days you'll send me a note telling me the good news!" I knew that they would handle whatever happened. They were good parents and such loving people. It would be a shame for them to be disappointed.

I had two wonderful hours with my neighbors that hot July afternoon. On November 29 I received a note from Pam: *Dear Lynn: We are expecting! My due date is May 6 . . .*

John arrived in the world on April 30, right after I returned home. And then I had a new "little" neighbor next door!

***

One Friday I was not expecting visitors, so I was spending time talking with Donna Holbrook as we sat on a huge rock. One of the trucks drove up and the officer asked our names. "Holbrook and Hartz," we answered.

"Hartz! You're who we're looking for! Come on and get in! You've got a visit!" I was surprised that the officer let me ride in the truck. That was not something that they did very often. I asked who the visitor was, but she didn't know. I had to stop by my room and get my I.D. card.

I was so excited. It was my sister-in-law. "Jamie!"

"I had business in Lewisburg and White Sulphur, and knew that I couldn't get this far without visiting you. So I stopped, changed clothes in a service station, and came right on over." She hugged me.

Surprise visits were so much fun because of the unexpectedness. We talked, ate junk food, and had a good "girlfriend" time.

Another surprise visit came while I was working in the power house. The telephone rang and Haggy was busy. "Lynn, go answer the telephone," he told me.

"Power House," I answered.

"Lynn, what are you doing answering the phone?" Ms. Marshall asked me.

"Oh, Haggy's busy, and no one else is here, so he told me to get it." I knew that my voice answering the phone had caught her by surprise.

"Well, I guess he'll be all alone now because you've got a visit," Ms. Marshall told me.

"I do? Who is it?" I asked.

"Well, I don't know, but there are four nice people here to see you."

"My church people!" I knew they were coming, but I didn't know when.

Two couples from my church came and we had a pleasant visit. They were out for a long ride on a Saturday afternoon, and decided to explore Lewisburg, after visiting me. They stayed about two hours, then went on to visit some antique stores in the area.

I wrote them later and told them how wonderful it was to have people like them in my life, to share the good and the bad, and how they helped to make something bad so good for me.

Strips and Searches

The officers have the right to strip search the women prisoners at any time. However, most of the strip searches are done when a woman is leaving the visiting room.

Donna Wells' husband and baby came to visit. She had a really good time playing with her baby and visiting with her husband. Donna embezzled a quarter of a million dollars from a bank where she worked, and she was only sentenced to five months in prison. Unbelievable.

When Donna was ready to leave the visiting room, the officer, one of the "wanna-be-lieutenants," decided to strip search her. This officer is obsessed with her power and authority. Donna had all of her clothes off.

"Now, squat and cough," the officer ordered Donna as soon as she was undressed. Donna did as she was told.

"Not like that!" Officer Hawk told her. "Like this!" She demonstrated bending, coughing, and holding her ankles.

Donna tried it again.

"No! No! No!" the Hawk told her. "You have to cough from here!" She pointed to her diaphragm. "Deeper! Deeper! Watch again!" The Hawk demonstrated again how to bend, hold your ankles, and cough from the diaphragm.

Donna tried it again at the same time that Officer Hawk was demonstrating it. "Here we were going 'round and 'round in that little room bending, squatting, holding our ankles and coughing. We looked like Simon Sez. I couldn't do anything to please her. She was never satisfied." Donna's vivid description of the situation with Officer Hawk made us laugh so hard that she had trouble telling us the story. "Simon Sez 'Strip!' Simon Sez 'Cough! Squat! Cough!'

"I had to wait to get out of there to laugh," she chuckled.

Child Care and Motherhood

Perhaps the worst scenario for all women in prison is trying to be a parent and having your child or children taken care of somewhere else, maybe by someone you don't even know.

There were several activities that the women could participate in that involved them with children. One of those was volunteering to work in the visitor's room with the children. Those volunteers were required to take training where they learned how to plan activities, work with the children, and provide an atmosphere of congeniality with the children and those women whom they were visiting.

One of the women, a Chinese-American woman, Lei, was married to a non-Chinese man who was a doctor. They had a little boy, Jerry, who was about four years old. Lei's husband loved her so much that he was licensed to practice medicine in West Virginia and moved to a town near Alderson in order to visit every weekend and let Jerry be with his mother.

I think the most difficult thing that I had to endure was my youngest daughter, Grace, going to Florida to live with her father. I was not able to be a part of the rest of her teenage years. She was frightened about the legal problems that I had. She needed personal and emotional stability, even if it meant leaving West Virginia. Having her with her father would not have been my choice, except that he married, and his wife was a responsible person. My heart hurt, but I wanted her safe. She did not need the comments from children at her school. However, if she had not gone, another sentence arrangement might have been made for me, instead of such a long a period of incarceration. Most of the time, though, I was glad that my children were not experiencing the things I was experiencing.

Read, Read, Read

I had always been an avid reader, but the amount of reading I did in prison was phenomenal.

When I left my home, I had five stacks of books on the floor in my bedroom. Each stack was a different category of reading material, and all of the books were new paperbacks which I had not read.

"Now, Mitch. Look. There are all of these books, and I would like you to send them in to me, a little at a time until I have them all read," I told him, showing him how they were categorized. There were a total of sixty-four books. I was not sure how long it would take for me to read them, but at least they were mine and did not belong to another person.

Mitch sent them in to me ten at a time, but they were not necessarily the way I had requested them. In actuality, I never knew for sure what I was going to get.

I could read up to three books a day, depending on what it was and how detailed it was. I read a variety of novels, religious and spiritual books, biographies, whatever took my interest. My roommate, Diamond, read. She received books in the mail, too. We read each other's books. Some of her friends sent catalogues and magazines, which we both enjoyed.

We shared our books with each other, as well as some of the other women in the cottage. For a while, I would send my books home when I was finished with them. Then I realized how desperate the women were for reading material, so I started donating them to the prison library. I bought the books myself and wanted to keep some of them, but compassion overtook my selfish attitude. I knew the books had to stay.

Some of the women were never as avid readers as they became while they were in prison. Ms. Harris, the librarian, told me that the books that I left were checked out and read sometimes ten times in a month or more. The paperbacks wore out quickly, but she managed to salvage them as long as possible. The women did not abuse the books; paperback books are just more fragile than hardbacks.

Diamond and I read and read. Sometimes we wouldn't say a word to each other for hours. It reminded me of Sandy, my best friend in grade school. She and I liked to be together. We would sit on her front porch, or mine, and read and read. We never said a word to each other, but we liked being together.

When I worked at the power house, several of the men liked the same types of history that I liked to read. I shared several books with them, and we would have interesting discussions about them.

The officers who worked midnights were not supposed to read while they were on duty, but I think several of them did. Some of them enjoyed the same categories of reading as I.

TV Time

As unbelievable as it seems, there was only one television for each cottage, and each cottage had approximately sixty-five to seventy women. It is impossible for all these women to want to watch the same television shows all the time, so each woman was assigned her own TV night.

That meant that about every seven weeks each woman would have the right to choose what was watched. Sometimes the women would trade nights because of specific shows or because something else interfered with their TV night.

There were times when there were arguments about who was watching what. TV was never very important to me, and I knew that I could survive without it, so I gave my TV night away. I did that by asking whomever I gave it to what they wanted to watch, then posting the list.

The biggest TV viewing was related to the O.J. Simpson case. When I was in Lexington, I watched the O.J. "chase," with the police following in pursuit. None of the women there were even remotely interested. There were shouts and cheers all over the campus when O.J. was found "not guilty." The only other TV program that drew as much enthusiasm was the Super Bowl, and any game with the Chicago Bulls.

TV I could manage without. A radio would have been much harder. A radio was the first thing that I bought, because I knew that if I could read a newspaper and listen to the radio, I could be satisfied with knowing what was happening in the real world. Diamond felt the same way. She enjoyed TV, but knew that she could live without it. She had earphones on her radio that could be taken off her head, and we would listen to the same thing together. At night I would go to sleep listening to talk radio, especially the Michael Reagan program.

Pets in Prison

If you think being in a prison meant no pets, think again.

People and animals will bond together, regardless of the life-surrounding circumstances. When I was in the Lexington prison, the women made pets out of the mice. They would feed them, watching them scamper about. I never did actually see any of them petted, but that would not have surprised me.

Alderson was filled with birds and squirrels and chipmunks. The squirrels were so tame that they would eat out of your hand, begging for more. They were smart, too, because they knew which women had food to share, and when to expect it.

There were crows that frequented the garbage truck that sat behind food service. One of them was aggressive, attacking other birds if they came around. I started called him "King Crow." Some other people heard me and started calling him the same. He would run off blue jays and tiny, little sparrows, as well as his own fellow crows. The hawks lived on the top of the hill around the health services. The crows did not cross the hawks. The hawks were no trouble to anyone, but none of the other birds went near their tree.

Animals don't know what a prison is, and the cats that lived at the prison were certainly no exception. They found themselves a rather luxurious home, considering that they were loved and petted (if you could catch them), by almost every woman there.

The cats made a home at the greenhouse, and some had found nice, little, warm, cozy places under the steps, or some other well-hidden spot. All of the cats were yellow-striped tiger cats.

One momma cat had a litter of kittens, which were immediately spoiled. Every woman that liked cats would catch them, pet them, and play with them. Dangling objects were hung from the tree for the kittens. Some of the officers adopted them and took them home. Ms. Patrick had taken kittens before and took some more. She couldn't bear to see them run wild or possibly be injured.

A new cat found its way into the prison. It was a black and white female with kittens. One of the reasons that women took food from the dining room was to feed the cats.

I was told that each cottage used to have its own dog, but they had not had dogs in the living facilities for several years.

As I was in the visiting room one day, I watched a pack of dogs go under the fence at one end, to get into the prison, and then they went out the other end, through another hole in the fence.

A stray dog found his way into the prison, making his home with us for a while. The women nicknamed him "Furlough," and fed him. He finally became tame enough to pet. He even recognized and responded to his new name. The officers tried to catch him and take him out of the prison, but were unsuccessful for a long time.

Furlough found himself a nice place to live. He had people to feed him and pet him, and he apparently found some place to stay warm and dry.

After six weeks one of the officers finally caught Furlough, and another officer took him home. I asked how the dog was doing.

"He took right up with my wife," Mr. Ellison told me, "but he won't have anything to do with me, and I'm the one who rescued him and brought him home!"

Another dog was found previously. The women called it "Stranger." One of the officers took it home, still had it, and continued to call it "Stranger."

Alderson is in the most rural area of West Virginia. It is surrounded by forest and woodland. There was a raccoon who found his way into the prison, spending time around the power house facility. He only showed himself at night, and the women working the evening shift would feed him. They called him "Bandit" and enjoyed playing with him.

However, one of the men, Jack Peters, set a trap for him, then took him out into the forest. Jack Peters was extremely disliked, both by the women and his co-workers. They missed Bandit and talked about him for a long time.

The Day the Bulls Broke in

My roommate, Diamond Kelly, had a visit from her husband shortly after eight o'clock in the morning. Carl had come to spend the day. She looked out the window of the visiting room.

"Look! There are cows!" Diamond said. And there they were, not cows, but two big, black Angus bulls!

"Look! There are two cows!" Diamond said again.

Ms. Starcher, the officer in the visiting room, came over to the window. "What do you see out there?" She looked out the window as she asked.

"Cows!" Diamond answered.

"Yeah. There are cows out there," she observed. "Who do I call?"

Diamond thought, *How should I know who to call*?

"Do I call 'yard'?" Ms. Starcher asked. Apparently, she called "yard."

Two other officers who were in the vising room got together and they all started to leave. Ms. Starcher ran to get her handcuffs.

Carl started laughing. "What are you going to do with the handcuffs? Are you going to use them on the cows?" The more he thought about it, the harder he laughed.

"I don't know. I've never had to chase a cow before," Ms. Starcher replied.

Meanwhile, these two black Angus bulls were running away from home. "Yard" came, and another officer in another truck. That frighted the bulls, and they started to run. Another officer picked up "Buffalo Bob" from food services.

It is important to know that "Buffalo Bob" works in food services at the prison, but he hauls cattle and buffalo whenever needed. He takes them to sales and shows, or delivers them to people's farms. "Buffalo Bob" would like everyone to believe that he is *fearless*.

At this point, there were two officers driving two trucks, and "Buffalo Bob" was riding in the passenger seat of one truck.

At the other end of the campus, Daisy and Donna were discussing whether to walk or not. Donna said she wasn't, because she had something else to do, so Daisy decided to walk alone.

As Daisy turned the bend of the path, she looked up. There was a big Black Angus bull, heading right toward her, running as fast as he could run!

Daisy thought fast and ran behind a tree. The bull ran right after her, knocking the bark off the tree, getting dirt all over Daisy's coat. If Daisy hadn't been behind the tree, she would be dead.

"His eyes were fierce, and saliva was dripping out of his mouth," she described to us later.

"Yard" and all the additional "yard" people, three trucks and six people, saw this scenario. "Buffalo Bob" got out of the truck and tried to get the bulls out the gate at the back of the prison. Instead, he was butted in the butt.

Someone working in the power house simply opened the gate, and the bulls left. A local farmer came to take them home.

"Buffalo Bob" was taken to the hospital for stitches. The next few days there were signs in the dining room about the "bull fight" and who won.

I knew the prison was a zoo, but this was ridiculous!

Contests

There were contests held by the recreation department for sports events, but they didn't interest me. What did interest me was a contest held by the Energy Conservation Committee.

For many years I have been concerned about natural resource conservation. The prison had a committee consisting of officers and inmates who developed ways to help conserve electricity and water. People in institutions can become very wasteful, because they do not have to pay the bills.

This committee sponsored a contest for writing about energy conservation. There were several categories: essay, performing arts, poetry. My mind started thinking of things I could do. There was something new for me to write and whet my creativity.

Jingles and rhymes to tunes of various songs popped into my mind. I began writing them down as fast as I could think of them. I had one for electricity, one for water, one for air pollution, and one for taking care of Mother Earth. I wrote it as a two-person comedy skit, with a joke for the ending.

And I won a prize!

The prize was monetary, which was credited to my commissary account, and an opportunity to play bingo.

I don't like playing games, but several of the women talked me into going and playing because there would be an opportunity to win more prizes. I didn't care about prizes, but I did go, and everyone won more prizes. I received several things, such as perfume and hair care products. I gave most of them to people who would use them.

The contest had occupied my mind, and I planned to expand the skit that I developed for another contest.

Special Events and Performances

Intramural sports events for the women were held by the recreation department. The most popular was softball. Prison softball teams also played teams outside the prison. The women who played were good players. They liked winning. There were also basketball games, but the activity that received the most participation was aerobics. There were several sessions of aerobics held daily and they were always full. The women who participated wanted to keep themselves healthy.

Piano and guitar lessons were also available. The skills were taught by other inmates.

Any time there was an opportunity, the women who liked to sing and perform would participate in the prison concerts or shows. There was a folk singer, country singers, rock singers, and even a couple of Spanish women who sounded like Selena, the Mexican singer who was killed.

The Spanish women did their own Hispanic Heritage Festival. It was as well done as any community theater production.

"Did I do okay?" my friend Carlita asked when she had finished dancing a Flamenco as a solo performance.

"Honey, you were great!" I admired the dress that she had put together for the performance. It was a navy blue, fitted dress, with a long train of ruffles. She wore high, wide-heeled shoes, and danced well.

"Irma, Marian, Lucia!" I hugged a few of my Spanish-speaking friends. "You all did so well! I wish I had the courage to dance like you all do."

Irma smiled. "I used to teach dance. I love it. When I get out, I hope I can teach again." Her long, reddish-tinted hair was brightened with sparkles. Her eyes glistened with exhilaration.

"All Spanish people like to dance," Lucia told me. "I miss that part of my life here in the United States." Lucia was a little chubby, and quite young. I hoped that she would get out of prison and go home to her family, where she belonged.

Later that evening I wrote Mom:

> *You would have enjoyed these women. Their performance was simply outstanding. I'm sending you a program from the performance so you can get a feel for what they did.*

My mother and father had taken Spanish when they were in school, and I had taken it in high school and college. We enjoyed the language and the culture. I knew Mom would be impressed.

There was enough talent in the prison to "take the show on the road." The only problem was that no one was allowed to go anywhere!

Love, Sex, and Romance

When I was in prison for less than a week, there was a sign on the door of the rest room that said: "Cukeless in Alderson." I wondered who had put the sign on the door, so I asked Ms. Payne, an older woman who did the maintenance on the cottage.

"Well, I think Ms. Billings put it there," she told me with a chuckle. She was a tall, dark-skinned woman with gray hair, and she wasn't particularly tolerant of people.

My curiosity was aroused. "Well, are you going to tell me what you know?"

Her smile got wider and wider. "Ms. Billings was searching a room and found a whole cucumber. She said she had no idea where it had been, so she trashed it."

I started laughing. "Well, I guess if you need a cucumber, you need a cucumber!" That was my first discovery of how women will meet their own sexual needs out of necessity.

A few weeks later I was talking with a Spanish woman from the Islands. Miranda was twenty-six years old and had been imprisoned in the basement of a prison, where she did not even see daylight for a year. She had been in prison in the United States for several years and was leaving in a few months.

"I found a way to make money while I was in prison," Miranda told me. "I made sex toys for the women."

"How did you do that?" I couldn't imagine even coming up with the idea, much less finding what was needed to make some such item.

"I'd ask the woman to give me a bra. Then, I'd take a toilet paper cardboard holder and I'd stuff it with cotton and cover it on the outside with cotton. I'd shape it to the right size and contour. Then, I'd take a nylon hose, cover it, and attach it between the cups of the bra. The woman could then put her legs in the straps and pleasure herself," she described the details to me.

"How much did you charge to do that?" I knew that she had made decent money, because she always seemed to have what she needed.

"Seven dollars," she answered, then added, "And they never hesitated about the cost." Miranda had found a way to support herself in prison. I knew that she could survive wherever she went.

One day, two women were in the dining room sitting on the same side of a booth with their legs wrapped around each other, playing with each other's crotch while they were eating.

Lesbianism was rampant. "Bull-dykes" is the term Lt. Stone used. "I just can't stand these women going to the visiting room, pretending to their families that they are straight, then coming back in here to their girlfriends."

Some of the women looked like men. Some of them were very much "in love" with other women. They would have "love bites" all over their neck. It was not pleasant to watch.

The women did develop emotional bonds and, when one of the pair was released, it was especially difficult for the one who was left in prison. Molly and Chelsea wanted a "blessing" on their relationship when Molly left. They exchanged rings with each other, promising to meet on the outside. I saw Chelsea sitting alone after Molly left, and talked with her.

"I'm doing okay," she told me. "I've heard from Molly, and she is getting an apartment. I hope I'll be out soon and we can be together."

Since the rules did not permit contact with a felon when a prisoner is released, I wondered how she would manage. However, knowing what I know, I'm sure they did.

It was also against the rules for the officers to have relationships with the women, but that doesn't mean it didn't happen. It did with the male and female officers.

Rumor had it that there were twenty-four correctional officers terminated in Lexington because of intimate relationships with the women. There were also numerous pregnancies after the women were incarcerated.

Gina Parsons, the recreation director at Alderson, was terminated one day. She had a relationship with another woman, who had just been sent to a halfway house. She sent her some money, which validated contact with an inmate after being released.

Furloughs

"'Bye, Diane. Have a nice time," I said to "Lady Di" as she walked over to R&D to be checked out for her furlough time.

"'Bye, Lynn. I'll see you in a few days. Thanks so much for letting me use your bag for my things," she said as we hugged. I lent her the travel bag that I was sent in to pack my clothes to take home.

Diane had been in prison for almost five years. She had a furlough before, but never one where she was able to go back to her home for a few days. She was delighted. Her sister came to pick her up, and they headed to Chicago.

Several women had been on furloughs, but none seemed any more happy than Diane. She was getting burned out by being in prison for such a long time. She had gained an enormous amount of weight, and sometimes she was just downright crabby. One of the food service staff told me that she was "short time" (getting close to the end of her sentence), and that the women sometimes would get disagreeable.

A friend of ours, Tammy Jamerson, had gone on furlough because her mother was dying. Tammy came back in a mixed, melancholic mood. Her mother had given her some jewelry, and she had spent time with her husband and children. She was glad for the time, but sad for what she was experiencing with her mother. Tammy had the option of spending time with her mother while she was living, or going to the funeral. She opted to spend the time with her mother. Several months later, the news arrived about her mother's death. The first person she looked for was "Lady Di." Diane could be very comforting and compassionate about human emotional needs. I was glad that Tammy found that comfort when she needed it.

***

"Fannie!" I called to my friend in the room two doors away. "You're back! Did you have a good time?" I knew Fannie had to have a good time. She had been in prison almost eight years, and her family lived in Florida.

"Oh, yeah," she said, with a big grin on her face. "It was almost too much to have to come back to this hell hole."

Fannie and I were the same age. She had been accused of conspiracy to deal drugs. She told me that she had never used or sold drugs. It was obvious to me that she was not a drug user. It was easy to tell after being in prison a little while who was involved with drugs and who wasn't.

Both of Fannie's parents were very ill and living in a nursing home. She hoped that she would be able to spend time with them before they died.

"Come on in, and I'll tell you about my visit home," she said as I walked in her room and sat on the edge of her bed.

"How are you parents?" I wondered if they were both still in nursing homes.

She said that they were. One of them knew her, and the other was confused. She was anxious to get home and take some of the responsibilities from her sister.

"And did you see Don?" I asked.

Her grin answered my question. Fannie had enough male contact that she could manage the rest of her time, keeping up her spirits.

Chapter 9

Friends in and Out

Socials

"Hartz! You have a social!" Houston yelled upstairs for me. I hurried downstairs with the newspaper in my hand. I knew who was there.

A "social" was a visit from another woman in the prison, as different from a visit from someone outside the prison.

I handed the newspaper to Sherry and Cheri. They said "thanks" and left.

"Why do are all these women come looking for you all the time?" Houston asked. "Someone is always looking for you."

"Well, Houston, it's like this. I get the only Charleston newspaper in the prison, and people want to read it. I give it to Sherry and Cheri. When they are finished with it in their cottage, they take it to the library."

"You know, it is really nice that you're so willing to share it," he complimented me. I explained to him how important the newspaper was to me and, once I had read it, I was finished.

"But some of these women aren't after your newspaper." He looked at me quizzically.

"Oh, Houston, you know what these women want. You know because you know things. They want to know about their life, and they know I can tell them."

Houston knew. He just didn't want to admit his own abilities.

What's Up, Doc?

My friend Donna, and I were sitting outside at the picnic table talking. Donna was a veterinarian by education and license. I was a psychotherapist with a doctorate.

Helen Trump came out of the cottage. "What's up, Doc?" Donna and I looked at each other and laughed.

"Which one?" I asked.

"What did you say?" Helen asked.

" 'Which one?' " I repeated. "Donna is a veterinarian and I am a doctor, too," I explained.

Helen chuckled. "I didn't know that. I was just being silly."

Donna and I talked several times about being the only real doctors in the prison. A few months later, two other women doctors arrived. Their charges had been similar to mine, but were related to Medicaid billing. Amanda, the older of the two women doctors, told me that she didn't even know what they were talking about when they accused her of fraudulent billing. DeeAnn, the younger doctor, didn't either.

The scenario was this: Competent professional women no longer able to practice their profession because of crimes that they did not even know they had committed.

"Wonder why there aren't any women lawyers in prison?" I asked Donna.

"I heard that there used to be one here, but she left," she told me.

A few months later I met Judy Pugh. She had been sent back to prison for a probation violation. She was a lawyer. She said, "I was convicted under the 'old law' and the probation can go on and on, and the only way to finally get finished with it is to violate and finish your time in prison." Judy was an older woman with salt and pepper hair. She was from the midwest and had no idea how long she had to stay in prison for the violation. Her violation? A sexual relationship with someone who had committed a crime.

"Inside" Friends

I spent many hours counseling people in my room or theirs, depending on the circumstances. One young inmate was talking with me one evening about a personal problem.

"Candy, do you know what I did for a living before I came here?" I asked her. She had chosen me to talk to because she thought I might be able to help her. She had no idea that I was a professional psychotherapist until I told her.

"Your story sounds so familiar to me," I told her. "Where are you from?"

"I grew up in Nitro, right out of Charleston," she replied. "I was raised by my aunt."

I could feel my mouth drop open. "Your aunt is Janet, and your other aunt is Sandy!"

"How did you know my aunts?" Candy asked.

"Ask them if they know me," I teased her.

"I'm calling them tonight," she told me. "I'll ask them then." Later that evening Candy came back to tell me she had talked to her aunts.

"Lynn, they can't say enough good things about you. Both of them say you are innocent of any wrongdoing, and then they said how glad they are that I met you."

Candy was sent to prison for marijuana use. She was able to get into the drug program, which would shorten her time in prison. She said that prison was the only way that she could finally be clean.

In January I wrote to my Uncle Fred and Aunt Macy:

> *I have so many stories to tell about what has happened around here. Sometimes I feel like Joseph or Daniel must have felt when they were in prison, and people kept asking them to interpret their dreams. I am constantly asked to do this and to tell people what will happen in their lives. People come up to me over and over and tell me that what I've told them happened just as I said it would.*

Suzannah

I believe that Suzannah Carder was the prettiest black woman I had ever met. She had beautiful, sparkling eyes, and pretty skin and always wore pretty lipstick. Suzannah had worked for the F.B.I. in Washington, D.C., and was accused of padding hours on payroll. She was sentenced to something less than a year in prison, and was going back to her old job!

Suzannah was a Chicago Bulls fan, and seldom went anywhere without her jacket. She handled the beverages in food service and knew more about how the machines operated than the staff did.

"Is Suzannah working today?" Ms. Patrick asked when she couldn't get one of the beverage machines to work right.

"I don't think so, but she'd probably come fix it," I answered. Suzannah came right over. That's the kind of person she was, willing to be helpful when she was needed.

I was glad when Suzannah was released. She was the first person I had gotten to know very well who had been released.

"I'll miss you, but I'm glad I've known you," I hugged her, tears pouring out of my eyes.

"Oh, go away!" Suzannah said. "I have cried not once, and now you have me bawling!" She hugged me back. We laughed through the tears.

Betty

"Come on, Betty, let's go to lunch." I hurried her up because it was getting late. Betty took care of the floors in food service and, if the floor in our room needed to be stripped and waxed, I always paid Betty to do it.

"I need some help on a writ," she told me. "I guess I'll have to get the law students to help."

Betty needed help because she was to be transferred to another facility to serve time for state charges. "I've been in prison before," she told me. "In one prison, I got to keep my baby with me and take care of her."

Betty was definitely psychopathic. She would not do anything to physically harm another person, but she knew plenty of ways to con, scam and scheme. I learned things from Betty that I will probably never need to know. She had no outside support from anyone. The only friend that she had moved and left no forwarding address.

Betty told me that she became a Christian while she was in prison. "I still think about bad things to do, but I won't ever act upon them again," she confessed. Her uncontrolled behavior now had a control mechanism. She cherished the Bible that had been given to her by the chapel, but she was unable to take it with her when she was transferred to the state prison. I sent it out to have it mailed out to her, but it was returned from the state prison, and she never received it.

India

"Can I sit with you?" a young, tall black woman asked. We were in food services just before dinner.

"Sure," I replied. "My name is Lynn. Who are you? You're new, aren't you?" I didn't remember seeing her before.

"Yes. I've only been here a couple of weeks. Can I ask you something?" She lowered her head a little.

"Of course. What's the matter?" I had no idea what was wrong with this gal.

"Well, you look kind of smart to me, and I wondered if you would give me some help with my school work. I've got to take the G.E.D., and I'm not sure I understand some of the work I'm doing, especially the math." She was honest and sincere about her problem.

I started to laugh, but I didn't want to hurt her feelings. "Who are you, and what are you doing here?" I didn't even know her name yet.

"I'm India. I was caught doing drugs, and I'm going to participate in the drug program. My mother has my two children. I need to get myself together, go home, and take care of my babies." She smiled, and this twenty-three-year-old told me about her family.

Every day after that we worked on school work. I teased her about picking someone with a head injury, who saw numbers upside down, to help her, but she learned quickly. She was amused when I told her of my education and teaching experience. It wasn't long before there were several other women working on their G.E.D.'s, who joined us in study sessions. India was one proud young lady when she passed the G.E.D. test. I was proud for her.

Opal

"Come on, Lynn. I want a picture with you before I leave," Opal Chapman pleaded. She was leaving the middle of October and the weather was beautiful.

"Gosh, Opal. I don't want my picture taken in this ugly uniform from food services," I protested.

"It's not ugly, and you look good. This is how I want to remember you," she told me. Opal and I had spent many hours together. I taught her how to use her own intuition to develop her own spirituality. She had learned about God's work in her life. I had learned some things from her, too, like how to smuggle in a watch band.

Opal's family visited her frequently because they lived in Washington, D.C. One weekend they brought her newborn grandchild over.

"Here, Lynn. You can hold him." She brought him over to me in the visiting room. He was so tiny and beautiful. I held him and cuddled him until I felt selfish for keeping him from his grandmother.

Mitch liked Opal. He had trouble believing that she did anything bad to be sentenced to prison. When I told him about her smuggling drugs into her son in prison, he was flabbergasted.

Lady Di

"You never did tell me your story about how you ended up in prison," I told Lady Di one day. We were sitting in food services on my day off. I was decorating her boots with beads and a lariat that I had sent into me.

"Mr. George, will you get us a knife out of the kitchen so we can cut a slit in the leather on these boots?" she asked the supervisor.

"You're going to hurt yourself," Mr. George told her, watching what we were doing.

"Oh, just get us the knife," Diane told him. "I've been using knives a long time, and I know how to use one."

He found a knife, and Diane promptly cut her knuckle. She pretended that nothing had happened while she continued telling me her story.

"I was living with a man for a long time, and he treated me really good. One day some people came to the house investigating him for drugs. They had a search warrant and went all through my house looking for drugs. I didn't know he even used drugs, much less was involved in selling them. Anyway, they found drugs in the attic, and I was indicted with these other people, as part of a drug conspiracy. When we had the trial, I was tried with people that I didn't even know and had never even seen before. It didn't matter. I was convicted anyway." Diane was serving a five-year sentence for a crime for which she had no knowledge.

"You know, Lynn, I get really attached to some of the women here, and then I feel so alone after they leave," she told me. Some of the women resented Lady Di because many of the officers and food staff liked her. She lived across the hall from a woman called O, whose given name I have forgotten. They lived in the same cottage that I did. Lady Di had the knack for fixing food in the cottage down to a science, and I liked to have her fix "prison food."

"I think it's so funny when you call it that," she told me one day when, she was fixing chiliquetas.

"Well, I never saw such stuff as the women are able to fix and eat around here," I told her. "Did you ever see any of this in the real world?" She agreed that she hadn't, either, until she went to prison.

"Not bad," I told her. "Really, really, good. Here comes O." I looked at Lady Di and grinned. O was a trip. O was as big as John Candy. She smelled food before it was cooked. She didn't have much support from the outside world, so people always shared with her. She was in prison for drug conspiracy, too.

"But I did what they said I did," she told me. She added, "I still don't think I should have spent as much time in prison as the time I was sentenced to do." I agreed.

Lady Di was one of the women who enjoyed some of the books that I had sent in. If the romance writers knew how the women in prisons crave reading their stories, they would donate a copy of every book they write to the libraries in women's prisons. I liked certain authors, and I had those authors' works sent in.

"I have some new books," I told her one day. "It is sure easier to get them sent in here than it was in Lexington. Hey, you never told me how you ended up in Lexington," I reminded her.

"I was sent to Lexington for a medical evaluation, and I was there for two months. There was someone there who was tried in my case with me, so they put me in isolation. While I was there, it seems that they 'forgot' that I was there. They didn't know when they were sending me back to Alderson. I thought I would go crazy with no one to talk to and nothing to do for days on end." She started wringing her hands as she reflected her experience.

"How did you finally get back here?" I asked. I already knew that the prison system was capable of losing people because the only important thing was numbers.

"Someone from here finally called with an inquiry about me," she answered. "I had to ride back to West Virginia with a lot of women in a van, and we were all handcuffed. As soon as I got back, Lieutenant Ball saw me. He said, 'Let me take those things off of you.' He has always been so kind. My hands were swollen, and I wasn't in very good shape when I got back here. Lexington was a nightmare."

"You know, some of the women that were transferred here when they made Lexington a men's prison, actually say they liked the way Lexington was run better than this. Rosie and Naomi both say that," I mentioned.

"I guess they didn't experience what you and I did," she answered.

One day Lady Di was almost dancing when she got off the telephone. "I'm going to be a grandma! I'm going to be a grandma! Maggie's going to have a baby! It will be born just before I go home! Oh, I'm so excited!" She was so excited that it was almost funny.

"What's it going to be, Lynn?" Diane asked me. "You ought to know. What's it going to be?" I thought she was going to drive me crazy.

"I don't know, Diane. I only know that whatever I tell you will be wrong, so I'm better off not telling you anything." She looked at me with the strangest expression on her face.

"Whatever does that mean?"

"I guess you're just not supposed to know until you know from an ultrasound," I told her. She finally kept on until I told her it would be a girl. When the baby was born, it was a boy.

Lady Di and I only had one problem. One day she told the people in food services that I insisted that Mitch stay until after count, so that I would not have to go back to food services and work. That was her perception, but in reality the timing was perfect for Mitch to leave after count time. We had that extra time together, and we cherished that time. When I found out she had said that, I was very distant to her for some time until I confronted her about it. She liked Ms. Jackson and Ms. Patrick so much that she just said that to them in conversation. Neither of them held any negative feelings about me for her comment. It was one of the things that made it obvious that Lady Di was getting to be "short term."

Ms. Rodriguez

Ms. Rodriguez had been in prison for eight years when I met her.

She was in her mid-sixties, and had been in prison for a crime related to money and drugs. She had been a very successful caterer before she was sentenced to prison. She was accused of rule infractions frequently, and would be moved from her room to the dorm.

"Lynn, I have something for you," she told me one day after Christmas. "I wanted to have them finished before Christmas, but I just didn't." She handed me three of the most beautiful handcrafted roses I have ever seen.

"Oh, thank you!" I touched the petals that were so intricately shaped. "How in the world did you manage to make these in here?" If she hadn't had materials sent in, what did she do?

"They're made from bread." No wonder she was always taking bread from the kitchen! I am still not sure of the exact process she used to make those roses, but they grace the bookshelves in my office at home.

"Miss Hawaii"

I was standing in the back of the dining room when a woman asked me to come sit with her. *This is like deja vu,* I thought. It hadn't been long since India had asked the same thing. *Wonder if this gal needs tutoring?*

"Hi. My name's Lynn. I don't know you," I introduced myself to the gal people called "Miss Hawaii."

"I had a dream last night, and thought you might like to tell me what it means," she said.

"How did you know I do dream interpretation?" I wondered if word spread about that.

"I didn't. I just thought you might help me." She was so pretty; it was a shame that she had one front tooth missing.

I told her that I constantly did dream interpretation for people, as well as spiritual life readings. "You must be gifted yourself, or you would not have chosen me so easily," I suggested. She smiled.

Her dream had to do with various rooms in a big house. She

looked around inside the house, in each of these rooms, then chose one room to be her room. I discussed personal self-esteem and choices with her. That was the first of many conversations with Miss Hawaii. She was sent to prison for a probation violation. She was caught getting on an airplane to go home to Hawaii from North Carolina without authorization from her probation officer. "All I wanted was to go visit my mother," she told me. I never did understand why she didn't just ask for permission to go.

Lorena

"Look, Lorena. You're stuck here, so lighten up a little. It could be worse. You could be somewhere else where the conditions are much worse than they are here," I told my young friend. "The nice thing here is the outdoors, and most of the people that work here are kind. I've been where it is worse." I described Lexington for her.

Lorena was a pretty, slightly heavyset, twenty-four-year-old Spanish woman who was sent to prison on a drug charge. She hadn't been sentenced to enough time in prison to do the drug program. All she wanted was to do her time and leave.

Lorena had a very negative attitude. I talked with her more than once when things were difficult for her.

"It could be worse," I told her one day.

"Well, I don't see how," she complained.

"Simple," I told her. "You could have been sentenced to more time. You could have been sent to a really bad prison. You are not dead. Do you get it? Change your mind, and your attitude will change with it. You'll be much happier." I thought that maybe I should go back into counseling when I left the prison. Then I thought, *This is why I can't work anymore! I am stressed listening to other people's problems, and there must be a better way of teaching people.*

Lorena loved my clothes, and they fit her. I lent her some things to wear before she had a box sent in. Then I left her a dress and some shorts when I left the prison.

Mona

"I need to talk to you," Mona told me one day. She had recently returned to the prison from the facility where the pregnant women went to have their babies. Mona had given birth to a baby boy. I thought she probably wanted to talk about having him cared for by her parents, but that wasn't it.

"There's another hearing coming up, and I'm afraid that I will be implicated in something else," she told me in quiet confidence that evening.

"Is it something that would be harmful to you?" I would have thought that if it were very bad, it would have been a part of her original charges. Mona was in prison for conspiracy related to drugs. She was accepted in the drug program and also the dental assistant program. She would be in good shape when she finished her sentence. *Too bad that this is the way she got help*, I thought.

We talked for a while. Her concern was relieved when I told her that she would not be implicated in any knowledge of the situation. A few weeks later she told me that she was cleared of any additional charges. She did turn state's evidence in order to get her sentence reduced.

Kitty Newcomb

I first met Kitty because she was a best friend to the woman who played the piano in the chapel. Kitty was distant with me when we first met, but she became open and receptive to my friendship when her marital problems began.

"My husband has filed for divorce," she told me. "He promised to care for my children, and he says he still loves me, but he is involved with another woman." This was an extremely difficult situation for an incarcerated woman to handle, but it was not an uncommon problem.

Kitty's husband seemed to play games with her. First, he wanted a divorce, then he didn't. He kept her in a constant state of emotional upheaval. We used the Bible to help her find an answer that would make sense and that she could live with. She did not want her children to remain with her husband (who was not their natural father) if he did proceed with a divorce. When I left, she was willing to accept his decision to divorce and make the best of her life where it was until she could leave and make a life for her children.

Jenny Cooper

Jenny had such a high-profile case that I had seen it on TV before I went to prison. She had run a nanny service in the Washington, D.C. area, and had nannies from England and Ireland come to the United States and work for selected families. Her problem was getting visas and passports for some of the women. She had some of them come to this country without the correct credentials, and that made her violate immigration laws.

Jenny went through a divorce, and was definitely manic-depressive. Her moods were manic when she committed the crime. She then became so depressed that she was nonfunctional.

Jenny's behavior caused her to be moved out of her room and back into the dorm on more than one occasion. She needed treatment and supervision for mental health. I wondered what good being in prison actually did for her. She tried for a sentence reduction so that she could go home and care for her children, but it was denied.

Carita Santiago

Carita Santiago was not her real name. She was in prison under an assumed identity. I never knew her real name. She was the young woman from Columbia, South America who sold drugs in order to have brain surgery.

Carita was so sweet. It was difficult to imagine that she could have been involved in a crime. The first time that I met Carita, she sat down with me to eat at dinner. We ate together many times after that.

"I have daughters older than you," I told her about Nell and Hope. "Then I have a younger daughter, too. If I could, I'd take you home and let you be my daughter. Your energy fits well with us."

From then on, Carita called me Mom.

Carita was a beautician in Columbia, and she made a living in prison doing hair. She had spent three years in prison when I first met her. She was cautious about whom she chose as a friend, and seemed to have a sense of who were good people and who weren't.

After I left the prison, Carita became involved with one of the new doctors. He fell madly in love with her and wanted to marry her. She disappeared from his life, and I never heard from her again.

Connie Handley

Connie was sentenced to prison for ten years for selling drugs. She had spent about seven years in prison when I met her. I liked her because her voice had a musical quality when she talked. She was bright, competent, and attractive. She worked as the secretary for the power house when I first met her, but shortly after Jack Peters found a way to get rid of me, she quit and went to work as the secretary for Bill Jenkins, in the electrical department.

"How do you like your new work?" I asked her a week after she started.

"It is a relief. You knew it would be, didn't you?" Connie sighed.

"I did. I am sure Bill is as good to work for as he is good to look at," I teased her. Bill Jenkins was a Kenny Rogers lookalike.

"I wish everyone around here was as good to the women, as he is. He is a gentle person, but really, really smart," Connie remarked.

"That's what I liked about being there. Those men were all bright, even Mr. Jones. It's too bad that someone like Jack Peters can get so much control, and ruin peace and harmony in a place that needs it the most." Connie agreed with me.

"At least I'm in a place where he can't bother me or do me any harm now," she said. I was glad. She didn't need any more hassles.

Gypsy Mines

I have no idea where Gypsy Mines lived before she was sent to prison, but she told me that her family were gypsies from Romania. Gypsy was in prison for drug conspiracy, but she said that she knew nothing about the drugs.

Gypsy had some kind of financial restitution, probably court costs or fines, and she refused to make any payments on it while she was in prison. Because of her refusals, she was not allowed to live in a room with a roommate, and had to stay in the dorm. She said she didn't care, and I don't believe that she did care. She did not think she should have to try to pay back money out of the few dollars that she earned in the prison. She had no other means of support, and the judge had not ordered her to pay the money until she was released.

"I think these people get to keep some of the money that they collect from us," she told me. I believed the same thing.

Gypsy earned extra money reading people's fortunes. She said that she was good at what she did. She earned a living outside of the prison reading fortunes. When she put down religious preference, she wrote "pagan." Gypsy had a way of irritating the staff, so she tried to avoid them as much as possible.

Nicknames

I never heard nicknames like I heard in prison: Chocolate, Kool-Aid, J.J., Peaches, Big Pat, Brown Eyes, Juice, Red, Ice Cream, Door Knob, Tall Girl, Spanky, Big Eyes, Pookie, Star, Cat, Bo Peep, and M and M. Staff had odd nicknames, too. Besides some of the ones previously mentioned, there was Robocop, Hef, Buck, Doc, and Brew.

The women called each other "girlfriend" more than I ever heard in the outside world. Diamond had a girlfriend send her a book, titled *Girl Friends*. She and I read the book, then we decided that we could write a better book than that. The other thing that women would use to refer to another woman was "ho," a shortened version of the word "whore." The word was always used in a derogatory manner, but not particularly unkindly.

Outside Friends

Most of my friends and relatives wrote to me regularly. Marlene Marshall, my neighbor from directly across the street, did not write. She was so distraught about what had happened that she could not write. "Lynn, I prayed for you every day. I prayed that you would be safe, and no harm would come to you, and that you would be able to do good work with the women that were there." I knew Marlene was so sensitive that she probably felt ill when she started to write.

Serious Problems

One night in late June, I had a vision. I saw my Uncle Glen with my Grandfather Richardson. They were sitting in big, comfortable chairs, smoking cigars, talking and joking. My Grandfather Richardson had been on the "Other Side" for thirty-three years. Uncle Glen had cancer, and I knew his days on earth were coming to a close. When I awakened from the vision, it was about eleven-thirty at night, and I knew my Uncle Glen was gone.

The following morning Mr. Hendricks approached me in food services. "I need to talk to you for a few minutes," he said.

I went with him to a quiet place. "I already know what you are going to tell me," I said, before he had a chance to tell me about Uncle Glenn. "My Uncle Glen died last night."

"Did you talk to someone this morning?" he questioned. "I just received the call a few minutes ago."

"No. I saw him in a vision last night, and I knew that he was gone." I told him what I had seen.

"Those things happen sometimes," he replied. He was becoming more accustomed to my "knowledge." I told him about me and my three women cousins visiting Uncle Glen in January before I left. I was so glad that we did that. Our visit had been pleasant, and I know Uncle Glen was happy to see us.

I wrote Uncle Fred and Aunt Macy about Uncle Glen's death. At the same time I told them about Jim Chandler's death. Jim had been a professor at several of West Virginia's colleges, and had worked for the State Board of Regents. I had seen Jim in the mall at Christmas before I went to prison in January.

"Lynn, the people who know you are so sorry for what has happened. They know you were not well represented or you would have prevailed." Jim hugged me. I liked and respected him. His life was difficult until he conquered his problem with alcohol. Then, just as suddenly, he died of a heart attack.

A month after Uncle Glen died, I received a letter from Hope. Will was diagnosed with throat cancer in the larynx. He opted to have radiation and chemotherapy instead of having the larynx removed. Over the next few months he became sicker and sicker because of the radiation. His weight dropped, and his throat was raw from the treatments. He did conquer the cancer. However, the first thing he wanted was a cigarette. Two years later, Will died of respiratory problems.

My Aunt Ruthie and her husband, who lived in Myrtle Beach, South Carolina, were going to a meeting, and stopped in Louisville, Kentucky to visit her sister and brother-in-law. While she was there, she had a stroke and was hospitalized. I was extremely concerned, but she traveled back to her home. She had a few problems, but recovered well. As sick as she was, she continued to write to me, sending me encouraging cards and notes.

My mother had medical tests before I left the prison. She was having difficulty with her stomach. When I returned to the Charleston area, she had more tests. The day that she went to the hospital to have an outpatient test, she was admitted and had major surgery, including a colostomy. She was allergic to some of the medicine, causing her to stay in the hospital longer than normally required. She was in the hospital for almost a month. A few months later, she was readmitted, having a heart pacemaker inserted. At least I was back in Charleston, when most of Mom's problems happened.

June Allen

Many of my friends apologized every time they wrote for not writing more frequently! My friend, June, didn't like to write, because she didn't want her letters to be read by the mail room staff. I told her that they were not read, but she still felt uneasy about the way the mail was handled. The closer the time came for me to leave, however, the more she wrote. She was helping me count the days down!

Christy, Ellen and Denise

June, Christy, Ellen, and Denise all became frustrated with the prison "rules." They each tried to send me things that were not allowed. Two of them tried to telephone me. Ellen and Denise tried to send me flowers for my birthday. Christy called to see what kind of present she could send me for Christmas. I kept telling people to just send me paperback books and I'd be happy, and if they wanted me to call, to send me a little money for the telephone. At that time the women were not allowed to make collect phone calls. All the calls had to be paid into an account in advance. Most people did not send money to put on the phone account. I simply could not afford to make calls to all of my friends out of my own money.

I never trashed any correspondence, not from anyone. I was amazed at how much I had accumulated. Ellen sent cards and more cards. "Need a hug? A great big one is enclosed!" Another one said, "You are always in my thoughts and prayers . . . and always in my heart." There were many cards like that.

Carla Henderson

My friend Carla Henderson sent frequent cards. One card said, "Sometimes when things aren't going great for me, I'll get a letter from you that turns my whole mood around. I think God put you in my life, because He knew what a positive difference you'd make. My relationship with you doesn't require that I be anything but myself, because you accept the real me. I want you to know just how much that means and that of the many blessings in my life, you're one of the greatest." Carla and I had been friends for twenty years. She had received a head injury, and I did not realize how bad it was until I was similarly injured. Carla developed migraine headaches. She said that she wished I was there to touch her head and cause it to cease. I knew that I couldn't physically touch her, so I drew around my hands on paper, cut them out as a pair, and prayed over them as I touched them, visualizing them touching and healing her head. When she received them, she used them.

"They work, Lynn!" Carla wrote. "When my head starts hurting, I put them on my head and it quits!" I knew that prayer worked. Research shows the effects of prayer on people and plants. The "point of contact," which is when a person touches something and another person receives that item, is one way of making prayer more effective. The paper hands were the "point of contact" for Carla.

At another time Carla wrote, telling me that she was more in a prison in her own home than I was in an institution.

School Faulty and Students

Some of my students and friends I taught with wrote to me. At times, I'd just get a note or a card. One day, I got a card with a note from all the faculty members where I had taught! I enjoyed teaching there. Paul Patterson was the one that told the encouraging story about "Sunday's Coming." It had stuck with me through all my problems.

He told me to think about how dark and gloomy the world must have seemed to people on the first Good Friday. All they knew was that Jesus had been crucified and died. They did not know that he would rise again, because they did not understand his message. Had they only known that Sunday was coming!" I knew that my "Sunday" would come. I just had to be patient.

Mitch

Mitch did not write very often. He usually sent me my money with a note wrapped around it. In one letter, however, he wrote:

> *Just remember, a whole lot of people love you and know that you are innocent, and they want you to know that. Remember, also, that at some point this will all be behind you and even if you aren't cleared, everyone that knows you also knows you didn't intentionally break the law, so don't dwell on that aspect of it . . .*

Another letter from Mitch amused me. Mitch worked for the power company and he had to go to a plant in Michigan to work. He disliked that plant. *The plant has guards walking around in riot gear and carrying rifles*, he wrote. *I flunked the psychological test to get in, so I had to talk to the psychiatrist* . . . . Even where I was wasn't like that.

Family

My Aunt Dodie sent encouraging cards all the time. She thought she neglected me, but she most certainly didn't. One card said, "Let your imagination take you to places you never dared to dream of." Another one, with Ziggy on the front, said, "Not only am I thinking of YOU today (Certified Thought) . . . I am sending you this card to make it official." One of my favorites said, "Things may be tough now. But you're tougher!" My mother-in-law wrote to me. So did Mitch's mother and his sister-in-law. How encouraging my family and friends were!

Mary Kaye

Mary Kaye was my father's cousin, and she lived near me. I didn't know her until after I was injured in the accident. We became friends, and she wrote regularly while I was in the prison. She told me much about my Grandfather Richardson and my father's early years. I told her stories of the women, and sent her encouragement and prayers.

Doug Likens and Bob Robertson

Doug Likens and Bob Robertson were both men that I had known for many years. Doug activated his church's prayer team in my behalf. He told me that God's plan was perfect and that it is difficult for us, in our humanness, to understand the bigger picture.

Bob and I had corresponded for thirty years. He was considerably older than I, but we enjoyed knowing each other. When I told him about my argument with God, he wrote: *I'm not a religious man, but I don't think I'd tackle an argument with the Big Man Up There . . .* .

My New "Outside" Friend

Who would believe that it was possible to make a new friend who wasn't in prison when you were in prison? My sister-in-law, Jamie, taught an insurance seminar and met Belinda DeMarco, a woman from Columbus, Ohio. They related well, and Belinda was telling Jamie about her quest for her own spirituality.

"Let me tell you about my sister-in-law." Jamie began to describe some of my experiences with the women in prison.

"Give me her address and I'll write to her," I told Jamie.

That began my relationship with my new "outside friend." Belinda sent me cards and letters of encouragement, and I sent her articles from magazines, whole magazines on spirituality and plenty of encouragement to develop her own sense of spirituality and healing. Belinda became involved in a church that works with prayer and healing. She has continued to learn various healing methods and techniques.

Although we don't correspond as much and still have not met face to face, we do keep in touch, and we still plan to meet.

Birthdays

Birthdays are special, no matter where you are, but it isn't much fun to think about having your birthday in prison. However, most of the women still managed to celebrate their birthdays with a party, cards, and small gifts. Although it was against the rules to give or exchange gifts between inmates and staff, it still happened. The staff simply looked the other way. Women by nature are nurturing and comforting, and small tokens of warmth and kindness helped make the experience bearable.

My birthday was coming up, and I was dreading it. I always found it easier to ignore my birthday than to confront it. When I was 50 my family had an "Over the Hill" party: black streamers, cups with black writing on them, black plates. They did it up right. But that wasn't the birthday I thought about as my birthday approached.

"Your birthday's coming up, isn't it?" Lady Di asked.

"No, it's today. It's January 27," I told her. "I share my birthday with Mozart, but I can't play or compose music as well as he did!"

"What birthday do you remember the most?" Diane asked as we were eating lunch.

"My fifteenth, I guess. My mother had given birth to my youngest brother, Andy, the previous month, and she still did not feel very good. I came home from school and started to put dinner in the oven. At that time Daddy had been working on the kitchen, and we still had a gas stove. I lit the pilot light for the oven, it caught too fast, and burned off my eyelashes and some of my hair. I put fish sticks in the oven for us for supper. My boyfriend had broken up with me at school, and I was quite upset. I knew he had broken up with me because he wasn't able to get me a birthday present, but I didn't care about that. Anyway, my mother had made me a banana cake with fresh bananas on the top. That was my very favorite kind of cake and, although she didn't feel very good at all, she had taken the trouble to make that for me. I'll never forget that."

Everyone imaginable seemed to tell me "Happy Birthday." That evening we went through the cafeteria line for dinner. I could not believe my eyes. We had fish that was similar to fish sticks and banana cake for dessert.

"Lynn, didn't you tell me today about the fish sticks and banana cake?" Lady Di's face had a quizzical expression.

"Yes, I did. Is this strange or what?" I answered her. "This is God's hand at work in my life. There is no other explanation for this to happen. It is God's way of telling me that He is with me always and, since my mother isn't here to make my favorite cake, His Divine Will made it happen for me."

Diamond wrote me a note:

Dear Lynn, Happy Birthday. Sorry you're not home to celebrate, but next year, and all the years ahead, you can make up for this disappointment. Besides, I'd miss you and who would braid my hair? I'm very lucky that you came into my life. At least one good thing came out of this . . . .

I shared my birthday story with many women over the next few days, telling them that I knew that God didn't forget me or my birthday. I had been in prison almost a year, and it was obvious that God still loved me, even though I had been angry at Him. I was finally beginning to understand how God works.

Chapter 10

No "Mon," No Fun

Pay Day

"Let's see if our money is posted yet," Diane said. "It's after 3:00, so it should be."

"Okay. Tell someone we're going to the commissary," I added. "Do you shop today?"

"No. You never seem to remember. I shop the same day you do." She was right. I never could remember that. I don't know why I couldn't remember, but I couldn't. Perhaps it was part of the head injury problem.

Each person was assigned a prison number by the Bureau of Prisons, and that number was put on a picture identification card. The card was used for shopping at the commissary. Depending on the person's identification number, a day to shop at the commissary was assigned, and those days were rotated quarterly. I never could determine why they were rotated, but it was just something that was done.

A short time later Diane received permission for us to walk across the sidewalk from the food services building to the commissary building.

She used the automatic teller machine, accessing her account. "Well, has it been posted?" I asked.

"Yes," she said. "That means I can shop tomorrow!" She was really happy. Diane didn't get money sent in from the outside very often, and she needed her small amount of pay just to buy shampoo and toiletries.

"I might as well check my balance since I'm here," I told her as I cleared the ATM for my own use.

"Oops!" I exclaimed. "I have more money than I thought I had."

"Where did it come from?" she asked

"Heavens to Betsy, I don't know, because I don't have any money slip for that kind of money." I looked at her, puzzled.

"Well, maybe Mitch sent your money in early," she suggested, because she knew that he always took care of my personal affairs.

"Mitch would never send me this much money, Not only that, I wouldn't want him to."

"Well, how much is it?" she urged.

"A lot, I tell you. A lot," I stammered.

"More than a hundred?"

"A whole lot more."

"Oh, yeah? I wonder where it came from?" she mused.

"I can tell you I didn't rob a bank," I gulped, "but I don't know where it came from. Do you think they made a mistake?"

"I don't know. Maybe they can tell you when they open up," she countered.

"If I have time to go over there, I'll ask them. I have to go up to health services to pick up medicine," I told her.

"Well, stop and get your mail and see if you have a money slip," she advised.

"Now that I can do," I smiled. "I feel like a detective in a mystery book."

"It must be a lot of money," she hinted for me to tell her.

"It is, but I'll figure it out." I smiled smugly. Most people didn't get much money in, and this was an enormous amount.

Later that afternoon, I went to the cottage to check my mail. There was the money slip for almost $800. There was also a letter with it from Social Security saying that I had returned too much money to them, and that was my money. Ironically, they had sent me more than I had to pay the court in restitution.

The mystery was solved. I could have bought the commissary

with all that money. The next day, I had my counselor give me the necessary forms to take the money out of my account and send it home. I had it sent to Hope, with instructions as to presents to buy for the family for Christmas.

Commissary Day

Shopping day for each inmate came around once a week. The commissary stocked various food items, such as crackers, beef sticks, rice, soups, cheese and salsa for chips, and snacks. They carried writing supplies, such as pencils, pens, writing tablets, and colored pencils. They also had personal care products, like deodorant, shampoo, and conditioner. They carried cosmetics, nail care items, and hair color. All of the items were listed on a form. The woman had to check the items that she wanted, hand the list to one of the workers, take a number, sit and wait while the items were being chosen for her.

The person getting the items would put them in a basket, call your number, then check you out. The woman then went to the cash register, handed the worker her number and identification card. The person working the cash register used the identification card to put the account on the computer, ran each item through the cash register, then handed the woman the receipt to sign.

The receipt had a list of all the purchases made, the amount, the account balance before the purchases, and the balance after the purchases. The Bureau of Prisons allowed each person to spend $165 a month, excluding telephone money, and the receipt showed the balance for the spending limit.

There was another way to shop, but the new warden, a man, decided to eliminate the special sales. There were several organizations, such as the NAACP and the Hispanic Club. These organizations held special sales that allowed them to raise money for special projects, such as speakers and other types of activities. Diamond bought a set of electric hair curlers from the sale. It was the last one that they had. They finished selling all of the items, and were not allowed to have any more fund-raisers.

Camp Clothes

When I first arrived at the prison camp, the women inmates were allowed to wear their own clothes in prison. Clothing was distributed through the laundry, and each woman was issued shoes, shirts, pants, bras, panties, and socks.

I had not had my allotted clothing sent in, yet. I had taken in as much as I could, so I had pullover shirts, my own bras, my own panties, plenty of socks, and my own shoes. My shoes were a problem. They were not substantial enough to manage all the walking that I had to do. Nor were they waterproof. The clothing that was issued was not bad. However, rules change at the whim of whoever thinks he is in charge. Women were not going to be allowed to wear their own clothing anymore. Some of the women became extremely upset when they found out they were going to have to wear prison clothing.

"Did you ever go to camp when you were a kid?" I asked Patsy Moore.

"Sure. Why?" Patsy answered. She would be in prison until the middle of the following year, and the clothing rules were changing in January.

"What did you wear?" I asked her.

"Camp clothes," Patsy looked at me quizzically.

Am I going to have to spell it out for her? I thought. *Can't she understand what I am telling her?* It was apparent that she didn't grasp the concept.

"Just look at these clothes as camp clothes. This is supposed to be a camp, and at camp everyone dresses alike. Camp clothes are what it is!" She smiled at me.

I knew that the main reason for the clothing change was to dehumanize the women more and strip them of their personal identity.

A Box From Home

I was expecting my box of clothing to arrive. It arrived as I was sitting outside on the grass with a woman doing some counseling with her.

The officer, Ms. Hunt, looked out back and saw me. "Hey, Lynn, R&D called, and you have a box to pick up!" I was so excited. I had waited until March to have my box sent in because I wanted to have summer clothes to wear. I had sent my list to Mitch, and he and Hope, my daughter, put my box together.

"Metal coat hangers?" Mitch had questioned me. "I would think plastic would be safer. That doesn't make any sense."

"Well, the women here are not supposed to be violent. The logic is that plastic would burn, and metal wouldn't. Remember, if it makes sense, do the opposite," I had told him.

"I'll go with you to pick it up," Jennifer told me. We found a garden cart and took it with us.

Thumpity, thumpity, thumpity. The garden cart was so noisy that it was embarrassing. When we started back, after inventory of the clothing, we were glad we had it. Each woman was allowed a box weighing no more than forty pounds. I had my clothes, the dresses that I had made, my shorts, T-shirts, and my sandals. It was warm, and I changed my clothes.

I felt so good putting on my own clothes. "Look, Ms. Hunt!" I told her. "I'm a normal person again!" How I wish, for the sake of the women who are still there, that they had not changed that rule.

Shopping at the "Mall"

Being in a prison doesn't curtail a woman's desire to go shopping. There are several ways a woman can shop: the commissary, the sales sponsored by the organizations, or the "mall."

The "mall" had a variety of items that changed frequently. Sometimes there were shoes, or sweaters, or books, or writing materials. There might be towels, toiletry items, a pillow, or greeting cards. It could be anything. But if you saw it and you wanted it, you had to take it right then because if you didn't, it probably wouldn't be there later.

The "mall" was the upstairs in each cottage! The best thing about it was that it was free! The women put out whatever they didn't want, need, or use. Much of the clothing that women wore was left by women who were released from prison.

The items went fast, so the women worked fast in order not to miss the "blue light special."

"Mail Call"

The mail was delivered to each cottage by the evening duty correction officer. The people who worked the afternoon shift in food services always were always late getting their mail, because most of the mail was distributed during the count, about four o'clock in the afternoon. All the women gathered in the TV room, where the officer handed out the mail. I seldom ever got my mail that way.

"Hey, Hartz," Houston said to me, "I'm going to make you go to the mail room and get your own mail from now on." I liked Houston. I thought he liked me. What in the world was wrong with him this evening?

"What's the matter, anyway?"

"Well, look here," he said, pulling the mail out of the bag.

"Well, what's the problem?"

"Well, look. This is yours." He showed me a huge stack of mail and ten paperback books. "This is everybody else's mail." He pointed to a relatively small stack.

"Oh, I see." And I did see. I had more than twice as much mail as all the rest of the fifty people in the cottage.

"Gosh, I thought you were mad at me or something. Aren't you glad I get the Charleston newspaper every day, and you can read it before I do?"

"Yeah, right," Houston said, as he handed me my stack of mail. "It's a good thing you and your roommate don't both get books on the same day. Most of this other mail is hers," he told me. "How in the world do you all get so much mail?"

"Have you ever seen what we mail out of here?" I didn't think he had.

"No, I don't think so." He shook his head.

"Well, you can mail our mail when you go check out tonight, and then you'll know how we get so much in," I told him as I picked up my mail, put it in a large paper bag so that I could carry it in one trip, and went upstairs.

Chapter 11

Rules Are Made to Be Broken

Smuggling

There were a great number of rules to follow, most of which made little or no sense. But remember, the prison is not based on logic, only the need to control.

For example, a visitor could not bring in anything for a woman to keep. In reality, many things were smuggled in for us. It took me a while to "get with the program." I didn't think about doing anything against the rules. I always followed directions. If I had not followed directions, however, I would not have been in prison.

"Opal, where'd you get that pretty necklace?" I asked my friend.

"My daughter brought it to me," she told me as a matter-of-fact.

"How did you get it in the prison?" I innocently asked, and probably appeared extremely naive.

"She wore it into the visiting room, and I wore it out," she explained. It was so simple that I had never thought about it.

Later, Lorena Dudley, a tall, attractive woman with enough letters behind her name to be in vegetable soup, was given a disciplinary action. Her room was taken from her, and she had to move into a dormitory room.

"What did you do?" I asked. She and I were friendly and spent time talking, so I wasn't just prying.

"Nothing. I was accused of something I didn't do and wouldn't even think about doing. I was in the visiting room with my parents, and they accused me of switching shoes with my mother. My mother doesn't even wear a size ten shoe. She only wears an eight-and-a-half." Lorena spoke faster and faster. This was one of her mideastern cultural traits.

"Who accused you of doing something like that?" *I wondered who would have even cared.*

"Ms. Hunt. I am filing a grievance. These shoes came out of my locker!" I believed her. Lorena's clothing was all nice, and some of it was rather expensive, I could tell. The shoes appeared to be quality.

"I like Ms. Hunt, but she's not really swift," I mused. My thoughts were, *I didn't know that was a crime.*

I didn't think I would ever try anything that might get me in trouble, but necessity results in recklessness.

I wore my watch in the prison. It wasn't an expensive watch. I don't buy expensive watches because I sometimes forget and wash them in the laundry, or leave them in a pocket, finding it six months later. The watch had a cheap white, plastic band on it, which finally broke. The commissary sold watch batteries, but no watchbands.

"Here, Lynn." Opal gave me her watchband. "It's not very good, but I can't use it, because my watch is broken, and the commissary doesn't have a battery for it."

Baxter put the band on my watch. I had to beg and plead, but he did it.

"Oh, come on, Baxter. I know you have a pocket knife with you, and I can't get this thing off," I whined. The officers really weren't supposed to do things like that to help the women, but some of them would.

"That one's not much better," he said.

"I know. Maybe it will last until I get out of here. Thanks," I said. "I'll say nice things about you when I write my book." He looked at me as though he were thinking, *Yeah, right.*

The watchband was fragile, and it didn't hold up very long. I didn't know if it would last until I could get permission to have one mailed into me.

The next time Mitch came to visit, he told me that he brought me something.

"Mitch, you know I can't take anything out of here," I told him. "What did you bring me?"

"A watchband."

We went outside. I took off my watch. Mitch removed the old band and put the new one on. I was concerned that there would be a problem getting it back in the prison because the band that came off was red, and the replacement band was brown. When I went into the visiting room, the guard had inventoried the watch as "red" on the list. I hoped I could get that band back in the prison. *What a silly thing to have to worry about,* I thought.

When I went back through the room to be searched, Ms. Hunt was the officer. She looked at the watchband and said, "The other officer wrote down *red.* That doesn't look red to me."

"Well, I didn't watch to see what she wrote down," I told her. "If she had asked me, I'd have told her it was brown." There, I'd done it! I told a barefaced lie, something I could never remember doing in my life!

And I wore the watchband into the prison.

I had learned to lie and to smuggle. Just think what going to prison had taught me! *I might really need to know how to do these things some day,* I thought.

The problem with the umbrella was much easier. I borrowed Lady Di's umbrella because she had two. I would walk around in the rain before I'd pay the price for an umbrella at the commissary. They wanted seven dollars for an umbrella that K-Mart sold for two-fifty! The commissary was a moneymaking proposition if ever I saw one.

The next time it was cloudy and rainy, or even looked like it might rain, Mitch carried a nice black umbrella to the visiting room, and I carried a raggedy black umbrella in. When he left, he took a raggedy black umbrella out, and I took a nice black umbrella in. No problem. I was finally getting the hang of smuggling.

One woman was caught trying to smuggle a diamond ring into the prison. She put it in a sanitary napkin in the bathroom. That wasn't very smart, and certainly wasn't the way to do it. She should have put it in the toe of her shoe, and then hoped she wasn't searched by Officer Hawk.

"Hooch"

Most of the smuggling was done in the dining room. The women would steal food and smuggle it into their rooms. A piece of fruit and all the drinks that a person wanted were allowed to be carried out.

Although the women were usually searched when leaving food services, much of the food made its way to the rooms. Rooms were searched for food, too, but it was usually very well hidden. When Jackie was my roommate, an officer searched our room and said, "I know there is food in there. I can smell it. Where do you hide it?"

Jackie just laughed, saying, "There's no food in here!" She lied well. The food was wrapped in the dirty laundry in her laundry bag, then stuffed back in the bag.

There was a legitimate reason for not carrying food out of the dining room. The cottages had no refrigerators, and the food could spoil.

Occasionally, someone would save up fruit, allow it to ferment, then make "hooch," which, of course, is alcohol in its most base state. Whoever made the hooch would find some place away from the cottages to hide the fruit, and then go back to that place for the indulgence later. It could be hidden in the greenhouse or around the grounds maintenance office, or anywhere that a discreet crevice might be found. The penalties for that were high, including the loss of a room and other privileges.

Destruction of Property

The rules could change as fast as someone could come up with an idea for a new rule. The silliest new rule that came along was that the women were only allowed one pillow to sleep on, unless they had something from the medical staff saying that they needed more than one.

I had two pillows since I was in the prison, and had even carried my pillow from one cottage to another. I was very happy with my two pillows, and I was not going to let anyone take one of them away from me.

My pillows were both feather pillows. One was considerably larger than the other. I decided that I could take one apart, put the contents into the other, and then I would only have one pillow.

I have mentioned before that I quit sewing when I went to prison, because it was just too complicated to get fabric and a machine. However, the commissary did sell a little sewing kit, and I knew that I could not be without a needle and thread. I mended many items, making things wearable for the women who didn't know anything about sewing. Now I had a real need for a needle and thread.

I split one of the pillows, then the other one. I sat on top of my bed on my bedspread, very carefully transferring all of the feathers from one pillow to another. Diamond sat at the desk writing and watching. "You're going to have a mess," she reminded me.

"Will not." I defied her or anyone else to deny me the right to my pillow. I continued transferring the feathers.

Feathers seem to grow in numbers when you're not looking. My arms got tired from the motion of moving the feathers, very carefully, from one pillow to the other.

There wasn't nearly as much of a mess on my bedspread as I thought there might be. I tried picking up the feathers that had fallen on the bedspread.

Diamond started to laugh. "I told you there would be a mess!"

"No, there won't. I'm not finished." *I dare anyone to take away my pillow*, I thought.

With needle and thread in hand, I carefully stitched the top of the pillow closed. I got up from the bed, carefully brushing the excess feathers from my bedspread and clothing. Then, just as carefully, I made a fold in the bedspread, then folded it again. All of the little feather scraps were on the inside. I carried the bedspread to the end of the hall, opened the door to the fire escape, and shook the bedspread over the rail. Little feathers flew everywhere!

There wasn't a trace of a feather left in our room. I took the other pillow and threw the exterior in the trash. I had destroyed "government property," but I had a decent pillow to use.

Giving Items Away

One of the other rather useless rules was that the women were not allowed to give their clothes away, or leave any for the women remaining in the prison. They weren't supposed to leave anything: pens, pencils, books, nothing.

Lorena Salud really liked a couple of things I had, and she was so close to my size that it seemed ridiculous not to leave her my shorts and one dress that she really liked. I left Helen Trump several T-shirts.

I knew that there was another woman, Loralinda Frazier, who was becoming really good using cards for spiritual insight. I told her that I would leave her my cards, but I wanted to teach her how to use them first. We spent several evenings working with them, and I left them, including the cover that I had made for the box, and all.

When I was checked out of the prison and had to go to the lieutenant's office, I was asked if I had given any clothes to anyone. "No." I'd learned to lie pretty well.

What I learned in prison was to steal, smuggle, find loopholes to get what was needed, and lie. If I ever needed to survive any disaster, *now* I could probably handle it.

Chapter 12

Politics and Prison

Internal Politics

There are two kinds of politics with prisons—internal and external. The internal politics were related to relationships that people develop, and how they used those relationships to gain power and control over others. That is the same kind of politics that occurs in any kind of business, because a prison is simply that—a business.

Prisons employ more people than General Motors, so there are politics related to the prison bureaucracy, as well as local prison politics.

Wardens would come and go, depending on the need of the individual to move up the "corporate ladder," or, in this case, the Bureau of Prisons ladder. Captains, lieutenants, and other staff personnel transferred in and out, depending on where they might find a better position, more money, and more power.

Another kind of internal politics evolved around inmate favoritism by staff. Certain staff did things for inmates, such as move them into better jobs or relocate them into a better cottage.

External Politics

Since the Bureau of Prisons is run by the federal government that is the control center. Because it is on West Virginia property, the Senators and Congressmen taken an interest in the prison.

Congressman Nick Jo Rahall was the congressional representative for southern West Virginia. My friend, Carla Henderson, knew Congressman Rahall. She introduced me to him in the late 70's. Because of my brother Andy's position in state government, they knew each other. When Congressman Rahall made his annual visit to the prison, I made a point of speaking to him. I wasn't sure that he would remember me because I hadn't seen him for a long time, and he wasn't the representative for my district.

He pleasantly acknowledged me and said he remembered me, whether he did or not. When I told him I was Andy's sister, he definitely made the connection.

I read the newspaper, and there were frequent editorials about Andy's programs, especially Worker's Compensation. In June 1995 a note from Sharon, his wife, said that the press was at it again—frequent editorials, both good and not so good! Of course, I had already read the articles and knew that he was under a magnifying glass.

The newspapers kept alluding to Cecil Underwood running for governor on the Republican ticket. Cecil was Sharon's father. He was elected governor of West Virginia in 1956. At the age of 34, he was the youngest person to ever be elected to that position. I liked Cecil. His wife, Hovah, had been very supportive of me, and had sent me an article about angels that had been in the Huntington newspaper. The note, dated February 6, 1995, the week before I went to prison, said, "I think of you often, and Cecil and I send best wishes and thoughts with Love and Prayers."

The Democrats were the strongest political party in the state. The problem with the Democrats was that everyone wanted to be "top dog," and there's not room for everyone to be "top dog" at the same time. The squabble began for the top-seeded position of gubernatorial nominee. There were other Republicans running in the primary, too, including the former astronaut, Jon McBride.

I think that the primary winners will be Cecil Underwood and Charlotte Pritt, I wrote to Fred and Macy in North Carolina. Charlotte was a friend of mine, but she hadn't had anything to do with me when the legal problems became public.

My prediction was right. The other part of my prediction was that Cecil would win the election in November, which he did. Since I was on probation, I was not allowed to vote. Andy raised money, campaigning vigorously for Cecil. I must have told more than two hundred people to "be my vote for Cecil." Even when I was still in the prison, I told the staff to support Cecil. The positive feedback from the staff was wonderful. One of the men told me that his wife headed Cecil's campaign in an adjoining county.

Cecil was elected with an overwhelming majority. Mitch and I went to the victory party, and then to the Inaugural Ball in January.

Meanwhile, Andy and Sharon were negotiating a divorce. The next thing that happened was Cecil appointed someone to replace Andy, as Commissioner for Employer Services. Andy was without a home, without his family, and without a job.

I wish I had supported the third party candidate.

Chapter 13

Goodbyes

Internal Punishment

It is very important to understand something: People are sent to prison for punishment, not to be punished while they are there.

However, breaking the rules can mean punishment. Different infractions mean different kind of punishment.

My roommate, Diamond Kelly, had only been in the prison for two and a half weeks when she was called to the lieutenant's office for disciplinary action. She had absolutely no idea what the accusations were about.

"First, they read me my rights," Diamond told me when she returned to our room later in the afternoon. "Then, they wouldn't allow me to speak. I tried to tell them I didn't know what they were talking about, but they just made me shut up." Diamond was a quiet person who would never cause anyone any trouble.

"So, what happened?" I asked. It sounded like some of the things I had heard about the disciplinary procedures—not very orderly or efficient.

"I finally saw the name on the paper, and it was for Denise Kelly, not Diamond," she sighed with exasperation.

"Did they apologize to you?"

Her look answered my question.

Jail

"Hey, Lynn. I hear you had a problem yesterday," Ms. Marshall called out to me. Ms. Marshall was a tall, heavy woman who was a fair officer, but she wouldn't put up with any infractions of rules or nasty behavior by anyone. She had served in the army for eight years as a "sergeant."

"I'd say. I don't know when I've ever been so mad at anyone in my life!" I acknowledged the incident, thinking that she must already know about it.

"Well, exactly what happened?"

"I was trying to get the silverware that was on a tray out of the sink before it was too heavy to lift, and that pretty black girl kept throwing food into the tray. She wouldn't step out of the way so I could lift it out. I finally got the tray out, and I was so angry that I threw the food that she had thrown in the tray into the trash. Then she turned around and threw food all over me!" I could tell that she already knew the details. "Ms. Aaron called the lieutenant. He came over to talk to both of us, but he didn't do anything to her. They don't ever do anything when something like that happens."

"Now, I'm a good one to tell you this, but you know that what comes around goes around, and that girl will get hers. I think she is just looking for an excuse to be taken to jail. Someone said that she wanted to spend the rest of her time in jail so that she wouldn't have to do any work," Ms. Marshall confided.

"That is one of the silliest things I've ever heard!"

Two days later I was again talking with Ms. Marshall.

"Do you remember I told you what comes 'round goes 'round?"

"Yes." I nodded.

"I didn't think I'd see it happen this fast, but I had to take that girl that threw food all over you to jail in Beckley last night."

"What happened?" I had not heard this yet.

"She got in a fight with another woman, and both of them went to jail. You know, I didn't think I would see that come back on her as fast as it did. Remember, I told you it would," she reminded me.

"I know. I didn't either. I'm glad she's out of here," I told her. "It's really strange that if you get in trouble in prison, they take you to jail."

"I know. I think it is, too," she answered. We both looked at each other and laughed.

She Didn't Say Goodbye

There are several ways of leaving the prison. An immediate release can come when a person has won an appeal through court. Another way is to be transferred to another prison or a halfway house. One last way is to walk out, not telling anyone you are going. The latter is not recommended.

"Count time!" Kathy Patrick called to the women in food services. All of the women sat down on one side of the dining room, while the names were read, then each woman moved to the other side of the dining room and sat there until the whistle sounded, clearing the count.

We waited, and we waited longer. "Recount!" Ms. Patrick called. Everyone moved back to the other side of the room to be counted again. Our count was correct. We knew that it was right.

We waited again. Soon there were lieutenants and officers everywhere, getting recounts. We waited again. Something was wrong. Someone was missing. This was not the usual "we can't count right" problem.

"Wonder who is missing?" Lady Di said. No one had any idea. It was late, and the cooks had prepared steaks for dinner. They were concerned about the food drying out or getting soggy. Count usually took about thirty minutes, and dinner was served about 4:30 or 4:45. It was after six o'clock already.

"Ms. Patrick, have you been notified as to who escaped?" Lady Di asked.

"I don't know who it was, but the lieutenants have determined who it is," she told us.

Denise Hock had walked out the gate, and kept walking. She apparently had a boyfriend who picked her up and took her wherever she was going. Several women were questioned as to their knowledge, but no one knew anything.

Denise was a "biker girl" with tattoos and a very dark tan. She worked with the electricians and the plumbers and wore the shortest shorts she could. She had told someone that she would not do all of her time in Alderson. She was convicted of bank robbery.

The police, F.B.I., and other law enforcement groups were notified of the escape. It was months before Denise was found. According to the newspaper, she was trying to get some of the money that she had stashed from the robbery. Rumors were that she was going to Israel and had probably left the country. I am sure Denise probably wishes that she had done all of her time in Alderson. She would have had at least five years added to her sentence.

About six months later, the same scenario happened. This time the food service workers knew almost without a doubt who had escaped.

Lisa Jensen was from Southern West Virginia. She had been in prison for a short while, and I do not remember why she was there. I think it was a probation violation. Lisa was emotionally unstable, and a diabetic. She kept saying that she was leaving because she couldn't stand it.

Lady Di talked with her, trying to help her through the situation. She spent hours talking to Lisa.

When Lisa was found, she was in an emergency room at a hospital in her area, getting insulin.

"She didn't even tell me goodbye," Lady Di lamented.

Releases

Besides being released because a woman had served her time and was going to a halfway house or home, there was also the possibility of immediate release. Although they were rare, they did happen.

"Paula, your case manager is looking for you," one of the officers told Paula Simms at lunchtime. Paula had her case under appeal, and a change in the law made her eligible for release for "time served."

She had talked about getting an immediate release, from the time she had been sentenced to prison. I liked Paula and, if anyone deserved such good fortune, she was the one.

A little while later, Paula came back to finish her lunch. She had to go pack because she had to be off the prison grounds before count time! She was going home.

A month later, Dana Jordan, received the same message. Dana lived in my cottage. She went to see her counselor, and packed faster than anyone I had ever seen! Dana had been in prison about four years, so she had a lot to pack! I wasn't working, so I helped her.

Dana's family sent her an airline ticket, and an inmate driver took her to the airport. Both of these women had the same judge and prosecutors, although their cases were drastically different.

Transfers

There were two ways to shorten the length of a sentence, but there were criteria for both. One way was to have been convicted of a drug crime and participate in the drug rehabilitation program. This could shorten a woman's time to a little over a year instead of three years, or whatever the length of the sentence was. The drug program was so popular that there was often a waiting list to participate. It was extremely intense. The women had to do educational activities and recreational activities. The program was well-developed, and the women were proud of their achievements. At the end of the program, they would hold a graduation party, and the families of the participants were invited.

It is a sad commentary on life in these United States that a person has to be in prison to receive this service. It seemed to me that such a program should be provided as outpatient treatment and prevention instead of incarceration.

The other option was to go to "boot camp." The requirements for that were to be physically fit and have less than three years to complete a sentence. I would have fit one category, but not the other. I was not physically able to do the rigorous work that the women did in boot camp. It is unfair that this program is available to some, and something comparable is not developed for others. But I never said that the government was fair.

Daphne Cervantes wanted to go to boot camp to shorten her time. She talked with her case manager, who insisted that she wait.

"Why do you have to wait?" I asked her.

"She said I wasn't ready," Daphne responded tearfully.

"What do you have to do to be ready?"

"I don't know. I have worked, finished my G.E.D, sung in the choir, and done Bible studies. I just don't know what else she thinks I need to do," Daphne responded, with obvious frustration.

"Well, you're not going to die here." I tried to lighten the mood. "Just keep on keeping on, and bug Ms. Brooke until she is so tired of you that she'll send you just to get rid of you!" We laughed. A few months later Daphne was on a bus headed for Texas and boot camp.

A bus! *These women criminals transfer from one prison to another by riding a public bus!* There is something wrong with this picture. If a woman can be trusted enough to ride a bus from one prison to another, does she need to be in prison at all?

Gwen Thackmore was another woman that I didn't care for when I first met her in food services. I had just been transferred back to food services after being in the powerhouse, and she didn't understand why I was so unhappy about the situation. She also did not understand why I had certain restrictions and would not mop the floors. She would give me the "evil eye" look, and one day she told me that she didn't understand why I couldn't do those things. I pulled up my pant's leg, showed her the scar, and told her to feel the back of my leg, where the back bone was still broken. From then on we were friends.

Gwen learned about shortening her time by going to boot camp, applying and leaving almost before anyone knew her. She was a tall, strong woman, and would handle six months of hard work with perserverence.

Going Home

Dearest Lynn, 12/21/95

Oh, joy, you are coming home! I can't wait to see you and hear your stories. I have wondered so much about what you were doing. The last I heard, you were doing that blessed work, for which you may have been preparing all your life. I know it must have been very difficult. In fact I realize no one who has not been there can understand just how difficult. But I know my Lynn. You have given Light to all you came in contact with. Please, please dear One, call me as soon as you get home. The loving welcome I will give you!

I am sure you wonder where was all that loving the months I didn't write. I'm not a very dependable writer at any time, and beside from that—well, you have no idea how glad I was to get your Christmas card. I lost—misplaced—something, your address. I asked Mitch for it, not once but twice, and I was ashamed to ask again. Maybe being blind had something to do with it. Up until October, I was so blind I had to be led around ... I went to three months of classes at Vocational Rehabilitation, to teach me how to live in an unsighted world, then, as I knew I would, I got my sight back. Well, half back...

... What a tremendous book you are going to write! I think it will not just be a book, either. I think you are going to do articles and give talks, and goodness knows what else. You have had such an experience but—like my blindness—I'm glad it's almost over with. Oh dear one, I'll be so glad to see you again.

Let me hear from you soon—and THIS time I have your

address in my computer! God Bless and much love.
Mechi

Oh how delighted I was to hear from Mechi! She and I had been friends for more than twenty years. I met her shortly after she moved to Charleston, and we both worked in social services.

In January 1996 I had a dream. I knew it was psychologically and spiritually significant. I dreamed I was driving, and I came to a place where I had to cross a bridge. There were three bridges. I couldn't see the one on the right clearly. The one in the middle was really wide, and had massive steel structure, both above it and below it, into the water. There were numerous cars going over that bridge. The bridge on the left was narrow, and it did not have any steel anywhere. There seemed to be no supporting structure where the base of the bridge was. It was arched, where the other bridge was straight and wide.

A voice said to me to take the bridge on the left. I asked, why couldn't I take the one in the middle? The voice told me that I couldn't change my path, because that was the way I was to go. I told the voice that I was afraid, because the bridge didn't seem very sturdy, and I didn't want to fall into the murky water below. (It looked like the Ohio River, after a terrible rainstorm.) The voice told me that I would not fall, and to go ahead across the bridge.

The car I was in disappeared, leaving me alone. The voice told me that I could go across the bridge on my hands and knees, and crawl, holding on to the sides of the bridge. I couldn't even see any sides, much less anything to crawl across. I told the voice, and He said to go anyway, and keep my eyes closed.

I started crawling across the bridge on my hands and knees, clinging to the sides with my hands. I kept my eyes closed. At one point I wanted to open my eyes, but the voice told me to keep my eyes shut and not to look down.

I couldn't wait to get to the other side. I wanted to hurry, but I was afraid I'd fall, so I forced myself to go very slowly.

When I finally got to the other side, I was on dry, solid ground. It was sunny and beautiful. I felt safe and tranquil. I made it!

The voice of God talked to me, much like God talked to the prophets. It *was* God.

The bridge in the middle with all the steel structure is symbolic of the way most people are going to the "Other Side." That represented the mainline churches, with all their structure. Most people need that structure to help them with their problems, and to get to the other side.

My path was chosen and guided by God. I could not change that path in the vision, and I cannot change my path in reality either.

The bridge I took was one not many ever were supposed to take, because the path was scary. The invisible force that held up the bridge is the Force of God. Feeling the edges with my hands represented the intuition that I was to use that as a guide. Keeping my eyes shut represented blind faith.

The voice told me that I would have dreams from that time on, and I would know that the message would be for me and others. I knew that I would never fear to share the information with whomever.

The other side of the bridge was symbolic of the "Other Side," and also the other side of my problems in the prison. I knew I would make it through safely on both accounts.

I signed my travel papers to go home on April 3, 1996. I was denied as much time in a halfway house as other people, because I told them I wasn't going to go back to work. The regional correctional people decided that I didn't need to have as much time there. I felt exasperated and antagonistic. I knew that decision was discriminatory, because I was considered disabled and was not going to attempt to work.

I talked to a few people from home, who contacted the West Virginia Advocates, but I was not contacted by them. I even called after I finally went to the halfway house, but they did not return my calls. Several months later, I read in the newspaper that a case had been won on the same kind of condition. I thought: *At least someone was able to do something about the situation and try to make it right.*

"Lynn, don't you 'merry-go-round' tomorrow?" my friend

Deanna, who was from Maine, asked me.

"Sure do. I'm going home!" Ecstasy punctuated my words.

"Would you like for me to go with you?" Deanna offered. "I am off tomorrow, and I'd like to."

"I'd love it. That way we can spend a little time together before I leave," I affirmed.

"I keep 'merry-go-rounding' with people. I went with Fannie, and then your roommate, and my roommate. I keep thinking that if I 'merry-go-round' with those who are leaving, maybe I'll get to leave soon, too," she analyzed aloud.

I liked Deanna. She had not been in prison very long, and I was still trying to figure out what she did to get in prison.

"I don't know, either," she told me one day. "I called the funding source for our project when I found some discrepancies in bills, and an investigation was started. Then I end up in prison for things that someone else must have done. I was told that I should have been on top of what was happening with the agency," she explained the best she could.

"That doesn't make any sense, Deanna," I told her.

"I know," she said. "Neither does your situation."

Diane was a native of Canada and was married to a United States citizen. She ran an agency that handled developmental disabilities.

"Lynn, I could never think of doing the things I was accused of doing."

"Me neither."

We enjoyed each other's company. She was a bright, well-educated woman, who enjoyed crafts and some of the same kinds of things I did. She had stayed at home during her legal problems, making and selling jewelry. She did it through one of the legitimate home business opportunities that sell you the supplies, then buy the finished product back.

So, we packed all of my belongings and took them to R & D. The officer who checked me out through R & D was one of the nicer officers who worked there. She didn't make me unpack and repack. She just had me write down everything, and that was all.

"Well, now where?" I asked Deanna.

"Next on the list is education." We walked to the next place on the "merry-go-round" list.

I handed the sign-off sheet to the education director, who was married to the captain. He was a nice person, but I could use a string of profane adjectives to describe her.

"Don't come back." She handed me the sign-off slip. I just looked at her. What I thought could not be expressed in polite company.

When we left, I asked Deanna, "Did she say that to the other women when they left?"

"Yeah. She's a real winner, isn't she?"

"She wouldn't work for me a day," I answered. "She is struck on herself and her so-called position, isn't she?"

Deanna laughed in agreement.

The following day my two oldest daughters, Nell and Hope, drove down to the prison to take me home. I had to go to R&D to be released. When I was there, I was given my Medicare card. I couldn't believe it! I didn't even know I had one!

"Why didn't someone tell me that I had this?" I asked the officer.

"It's considered a form of identification, and you're not allowed to have it," she said smartly.

"That's not what I asked. I asked why I wasn't notified that it was here," I told her.

"We don't have to tell you these things," she retorted.

"I'm not so sure that's true," I answered her. She didn't say any more.

I was driven to the gate in the same way I had been picked up from the gate. My daughters were there, waiting. The officer who had driven me to the gate was friendly and helpful in getting my things in Hope's car.

"'Bye! Have a safe trip!" She waved as we left.

"She seemed nice," Nell said.

"Yes, she is," I answered. "I wondered who would be the last person from the prison that I would see, and I was hoping it would be someone nice."

The drive home was also nice. We talked all the way. It had been such a long time since I had been in an automobile that I felt motion sickness. We stopped a couple of times and then stopped to eat. I felt relief to be away. If I had known what was coming, however, I think I would have stayed and not gone to the halfway house.

Halfway Houses

"Halfway house" is the colloquial for "community correctional center." These are not run by the federal government, but are, in essence, contracted to corporations or individuals. Some of them are run more like prisons, others are more relaxed atmospheres. All of them have people who are correctional officer wanna-bes.

Because these facilities are contracts, the management of them may or may not be standard. I thought the prison was a crazy place until I went to the halfway house.

The halfway house where I was assigned was in what is now called Jefferson, West Virginia. Jefferson was recently incorporated, and it sits on Route 60, between St. Albans and South Charleston. That particular area is known for its strip joints and topless bars. *A truly fine location for such an institution,* I thought.

The director was a rather nice woman, Kitty Black. She wanted things done right, and she was quite courteous to me. Her husband also worked there, and he was arrogant.

Shortly after I arrived, I wrote my sister, Jean. "I do not like being here at all. This place is dirty, nasty, and noisy. The food here is horrible. In many ways I wish I had stayed in Alderson until May 28."

I was given a roommate, Patsy Smith, who stole my medicine. I finally asked to have my medicine locked in the office, and then all havoc broke loose. Patsy was taken to jail, but not until she had taken all my medicine and flushed it down the toilet. She is one who will end up in prison permanently.

While I was in the halfway house, I was able to go to my own church. What a blessing that was. I had missed my church and the church family. We had a new minister, and I could hardly wait to meet him and his family.

There were some extremely inconsiderate people working in the halfway house. When I was allowed to go home, they had to call and check to see if I was there. I did not mind that, but I did mind being called at 3:00 in the morning, just to see if I were home. They could have called earlier in the shift. However, people who need power and control over other people will use it, just because they can. I began to feel very sorry for these people. They must be miserable on the inside.

Mitch hated the halfway house and avoided spending any time with me there. My sister Joanne's companion, Bill, came several evenings, brought me a cola and sat and talked. Joanne brought me my first home-cooked food. It was good to be "almost" home. I anticipated being finished with the whole ordeal.

Probation

I was assigned a probation officer to monitor the "supervised release." Mitch and I had heard about her from a friend of hers, who became a correctional officer at the prison.

Sarah McCorkle and I liked each other immediately. The problem was that she was married to Mitch's cousin. Although she had never met Mitch, the court thought that someone else should be assigned to me.

Sarah and Don Winkler came to my house. Both of them were aware of how angry I was about the situation. "I hope that I never have to go anywhere near the federal building ever in my whole life!" I told them. I could feel the hostility rising as I spoke.

They must have understood, because I never had to go there for any purpose. All I had to do was complete a form once a month and mail it in.

***

"Did you send that paper in to the probation office?" Mitch asked.

"Sent it in a couple of days ago," I affirmed.

"How long do you have to do that?"

"Oh, another year, I guess."

"That is so silly. It's just some way that the government can keep control of what you're doing and how much money you have. Every time I think about it, I get angry." And I noticed that his red face affirmed his anger.

"I've tried to get a lawyer to handle getting me off probation, but he said he didn't know what to do or how, so if anything gets done, I'll have to do it myself," I told him.

"That judge won't do it," Mitch stated.

"Maybe not, but all I can do is try. Meanwhile, I'll just keep sending in that paper every month. I am glad that I have a person who doesn't bother me or that I don't have to be available to do urine tests or anything," I commented.

"I think I'll write the judge and tell him I want to be off probation, so that I can vote in the next election," I told Mitch. "That is the only big problem with being on probation now."

"He won't do it. He doesn't like you," Mitch said.

"I know. That's what Don said. It was obvious during the trial that he didn't like me. What else is new? All he can do is say 'No,' " I answered.

On September 24, 1998, I received a release from Judge Harper. I was no longer on probation!

At last, nine and a half years after the investigation had started, this was over. I was finally legally free.

Chapter 14

Total Freedom

I found freedom long before I left the prison.

Before I went to the prison, my friend, Ray Landers, wrote me a "Message from God."

This is a day that the Lord hath made. I will rejoice and be glad in it. Today is the day to rejoice in the Lord. Look about you. See the beauty of the world that I have created. All things that I have created are beautiful. This includes you. I have created you for a reason. You do have a purpose. I have heard your cries and seen your tears. This day I hold you in the palm of my hand. All things happen for a reason. I realize that you don't understand all that you have been exposed to. Continue to trust in me. You have not been deceived. I will accomplish all that I have set out to accomplish. Faith cometh by hearing, and hearing by the word. Continue to trust in my word. It has gone forth. Many times have I spoken to you. I have my hand upon you. I do have a work for you. Again, I say, look about you. Feast your eyes upon the beauty in your life, the things and the people which you hold dear. There are those who love you and respect you. This has not been taken away from you. The love is still there. Absorb this love. Bask in this love which surrounds you. My hands are upon you. Trust in me. Don't give up. When things look darkest, look for the light. For there is light at the end of the tunnel. Remember, you are not alone. Look up from whence your help comes.

Trust in yourself. I have given you abilities which others desire. Trust in these abilities. They will not fail you. Again, I say, Trust.

Trust

My argument with God ended long before I left the prison. I used to say that I wanted God to walk in my shoes. It had never occurred to me that I wanted God to walk in my shoes, but only where I wanted to go. By having that in my mind, I was limiting God. I was telling God how to do His work. I was also limiting myself and my relationship with God.

When Christ said "Follow me" to his disciples, some of them said they had to do one thing or another, and there were excuses about so much. I had been guilty of saying, "I will follow, but only certain places."

As I worked on my manuscript about people in prison, I began to feel ashamed of myself, because I did not have to endure the miseries that the people I wrote about did. I was not a prisoner of war. I was not tortured, beaten, stripped of my clothing, or raped. I was not burned at the stake like Joan of Arc. What happened to me was unfair, but I am not the only person that unfair things have happened to. It was not fair that prisoners of war were treated badly, or even killed.

Trusting God means that we know His Spirit is always with us, and that knowledge and belief is the strength that will help us through any adversity. I thought that I had experienced enough in my life and that I trusted God completely, but setting limits on God is not complete trust. Why I had to have an example of such a lesson in trust has yet to be fully revealed to me, but I have no doubt that I needed that knowledge in that form in order to do God's work.

When we "Follow Him," our spirit needs to be receptive to wherever His Spirit takes us, even if it is into the prisons or the middle of a battle field with artillery all around us. The Apostle Paul felt the need to go to Rome to preach the good news. He went as a prisoner in order to get there.

Then I remembered the story of Jonah. He spent three days in the belly of a big fish because he didn't want to go where God was sending him. In Mideastern language, that is symbolic of being in a big mess or in a "pickle." Jonah wanted to go where Jonah wanted to go, not where he was being sent.

One night, when I had only been in the prison for a week, I had a dream that I was hanging on a rock cliff. My Uncle Fred was hanging on, too, but he could get down. I was afraid of falling. Finally, I found a place to put my foot, and I could climb over to a family's porch, but it was flooded. I had to walk in water to get through, and when I got to the other side, my family was there having a picnic. The children were picking at their food, and my cousin who had been ill was healed. I felt physically alone, but wasn't.

The rock cliff symbolized my life with God, and how I felt—unsure of what kind of a grip I had on it. Uncle Fred was symbolic of the guidance and wisdom that I needed. I knew that the problems and feelings I had were very deep, but I would get through them, and they were not as deep as they first appeared. I would return to my family in the springtime, and we would be able to have good times again. I knew my cousin was healed, although she wasn't as healthy as she would like to be. Other things would return to normal.

No matter what happened in my life, I knew that I would probably always be alone. People who follow the kind of spiritual path that I follow often are alone. That does not mean lonely. It means the ability to be a whole person without depending on anyone other than God. Some monks, priests, and nuns are like that. I believed that my time in prison was part of the development of the process of internal, spiritual wholeness.

The message of trust is simple: *Life is not always fair, but God is always there.*

Whether things just happen randomly, or if they are chosen as specific experiences for each individual, is not important. What is important is that we trust God to lead us through the "valley of the shadow" *without* fear. When we take our eyes off the path and our hand out of God's, we let the human traits of anger, anxiety, and doubt creep in, separating us from our oneness with Him.

Faith

It is important to understand the differences between belief and faith. Belief is a thinking process in the cognitive part of the left side of our brain. Faith is an emotional process that is right-brained.

It is normal for the cognitive part of our brain to question what happens in our lives on an intellectual level. Those thoughts are important, because the cognitive part of our brain is orderly, and it is important to find answers to things that are illogical, or senseless.

In his book, *When Heaven Is Silent*, Ronald Dunn said that it is possible to trust God and still get hurt. When this happens, the emotional side of our brain reacts, and we feel abandoned by God. Without the element of faith, a person can become bitter.

I believe that it is healthy to question the mind of God, because the intellectual reasoning, or lack of reason, will inevitably lead to a spiritual response. That response is always the same. *Faith.*

There is an old hymn called "Faith is the Victory." It says that "Faith is the victory that overcomes the world." In other words, faith is the essential quality to living with things in life that do not make sense to us intellectually.

The search for God's love through the difficult times in life, brings peace and joy because in searching, God can always be found. God doesn't hide. God doesn't abandon us. God is always with us. All we have to do is look for Him, and we will find His love, peace, and comfort, because He lives within our hearts and souls.

Forgiveness

The humanness in each of us has difficulty with forgiveness. I am sure each of us would like to be more like Jesus as he was dying on the cross and said, "Father, forgive them, for they know not what they do." He was not doing anything *to* the people who crucified Him. He was purging himself of resentment, bitterness, and possibly even hate. The ability to forgive is not a quality that we need to do for someone else. It is something that we need to do for ourselves. When we forgive our enemies, whatever they did to us can no longer harm us.

Jack Kornfield related a story of two ex-prisoners of war. One asked another, "Have you forgiven your captors yet?" The other one relied, "No, never." The first one told him, "Then it seems like they still have you in prison, don't they?"

Forgiveness has to happen in order for us to be whole and spiritually healthy. Holding on to the negativity of circumstances and situations, keep us from our connection with God.

I have forgiven those people who have harmed me, lied about me, and unjustly imprisoned me. I am now able to say the same thing as Joseph did when his brothers realized whom he was in Egypt. They had put him in a well and left him for dead. Then, Joseph was in prison in Egypt for crimes he didn't commit. Joseph told his brothers, "You meant it for evil, but God meant it for good."

Wisdom and Truth

I love and admire the Dalai Lama and the Buddhist monks. They seem to have the wisdom of the ages in the depths of their souls. In an interview by T. George Harris, he quotes the Dalai Lama:

> *One of my closest friends spent, I think, eighteen years in Chinese prison and labor camps. In the early 80's they allowed him to come to India. On occasion he and I discuss his experiences in various Chinese labor camps. And he told me that during those period, on a few occasions he really faced some danger. I asked what kind of danger and his response was, "Oh, danger of losing compassion for the*

Chinese."

That kind of mental attitude is, I believe, a key factor to sustain peace of mind.

We pray, "Thy will be done," in the prayer that Jesus taught us. All too often, though, we really don't want God's will. That is why we need to pray that prayer. It brings us back to the consciousness of God's Divine Will in our lives.

Understanding divine wisdom and truth lead us to trust and faith. Then, and only then, can we be totally free.

Total Freedom

All of the above components were questioned, analyzed, and scrutinized by me over and over while I was in prison. I did not want to understand. I only wanted to be free.

Then I became aware. Awareness is the key to freedom. I became aware of various other kinds of prisons that people make for themselves. Some people are bound up in emotional negativity, which is a state of personal imprisonment. Other people are in work situations that are prisons, either physically or emotionally. Still others become enslaved to money, power, fame, or fortune. Those prisons can be worse than a physical prison, with chains and bars.

Charles Colson, founder of Prison Fellowship, described a prison in Sao Jose dos Campos, in Brazil. It is operated by Prison Fellowship as an alternative prison. It is run on the Christian principles of love. There are only two full-time staff persons. Everything else is done by the 730 inmates, serving time for charges of murder, robbery, and drugs. Mr. Colson described the inmates as smiling, and the men were at peace. The prison was clean, and the men worked industriously.

One of the guides escorted him to a cell that had been used for solitary confinement. The guide put his key in, asking Mr. Colson if he wanted to go in. Of course, he did. The prisoner in that cell was a crucifix—Jesus, hanging on the cross.

"He's doing time for the rest of us," the guide told him.

I found the same kind of freedom in prison that those men found. Freedom is in the mind, the heart, and the soul. It is nowhere else. No one can take it from you. It is a gift from God, and it is offered to everyone. All we have to do is accept it. It is free.

And I am totally free.

Epilogue

Although we can learn to find internal peace and personal freedom in situations that are morally wrong, that does not excuse the fallibility of a system that created such a problem. It would be as immoral as excusing Nazism or the Holocaust.

When we as people know there is something amiss in our society and our world, we have a responsibility to attempt to correct the problem, not rationalize it or accept it as it is.

The judicial system has been a problem for the United States since its conception. Thomas Jefferson's greatest concern for the constitution of the United States was the legal system. His concern was that it had too much control, and there were not enough cheques and balances on the system.

The incarceration of the numbers of human beings in the United States amounts to warehousing people. This is unconscionable. The United States, the "land of the free and the home of the brave," imprisons more of her population than any other country in the world. What is wrong with this picture?

Several things. First, the legal system does not work in all situations because of the internal politics of lawyers and the Department of Justice. A friend of mine was telling me about sitting in a bar listening to two lawyers discuss a case. One was the prosecutor and the other was a defense lawyer for an individual. They were discussing how they were going to handle this client and what kind of a deal they were going to cut. I believe these "deals" are made frequently and usually without the client's involvement. The legal client is simply a pawn for those people who play this power game. It is morally wrong.

Second, the jury system certainly needs to be reformed. It is usually not a jury of your "peers," but rather ordinary citizens who have the right to vote. That is all.

Thirdly, the real problems of society that bring the legal system into the world of the people have yet to be addressed. The problems are not guns and drugs. That is the symptom of the problems. The real problems are greed, power, and control. The other problem is inadequate education.

When I refer to greed, I am referring to "big business America," where there is more money than imaginable, and people are employed for minimum wage or given part-time jobs with no benefits. There is enough money in this world for everyone to live comfortably, but until a decent wage is given, not because the law says it is the minimum, but because it is the right thing to do, we can expect money crimes to continue.

Drugs are a money crime. It is not the drugs that are the problem nearly as much as the money that is involved. Oh, I am not minimizing the use of drugs; I am simply saying that the distribution of drugs in because of a lack of legitimate money, not because people need drugs (the product).

Even solving the problems on a social level by incarcerating people is not the answer. There are many other solutions that need to be considered. Do people who have a problem with drugs need help? Yes. Do they need to be in a prison to get that help? No. Do people who embezzle or commit a fraud related to money need help? Yes. Do they need to be incarceratead to receive that help? No.

Perhaps you are getting a better understanding of the social and legal problem.

Prisons are big business in the United States. They employee more people than General Motors. That alone should be waving a red flag in our faces, telling us that there is something wrong.

Wheeling and dealing over another human's life is morally wrong. Incarcerating people in order to keep the prison system running is corrupt. Having people pass judgement on another person without providing an adequate defense is as dishonorable as killing another person without that person being able to defend him or herself.

Do I have the answers or solutions to this problem? No. However, I know that there are some answers and as a collective group of people those answers can be found. The answers can only be found if the citizens of this country care enough to make the necessary changes in government and judicial reform. If we don't, you could be the next person in prison for something you did not do or know anything about.

And, if nothing changes, each of us in this United States is responsible, because we did nothing. I, for one, do not want to carry that burden. Let us find the truth, and let the truth set the prisoners of America free.

Together, as a society, we can change the world.

APPENDIX A

Poetry Written in and About Prison

SIX BY NINE PRISON ROOM

In this space of six by nine
Two people live together just fine.
One sleeps low and one sleeps high
In this small space we just get by.

There's not much room in this small space
But all our possessions have their own place.
Books on the shelf and shoes on the floor
Clothes on the rod and a mirror on the door.

A desk and two lockers, thing under the bed,
Plants in the window, nothing else instead.
Laundry on the hooks, food in the lockers,
Two rugs grace the floor in bright colors.

Photos on the bulletin board and a calender on the desk
A place for coffee, mugs, and personal items to rest.
No space to turn around for two in a room
It's only for a short time, and then we'll go home.

RIGHT HERE, RIGHT NOW

This is the present right here, right now.
All is well.

This is the moment, the time, right now.
This is all I have.

I live in the moment, the present, today.
All is enough.

Today is complete, the moment is now.
Tomorrow will take care of itself.

Catch the moment, it doesn't last long.
Cherish your time.

Always.

I WANT TO KNOW GOD

Oh, God, I want to know you in my pain and in my sorrow.
I want to know you more now than waiting for tomorrow.
I want to know you in the good times and the bad
And feel your mighty presence when things in life are sad.
I want to know you deeply within my heart and soul
And feel your manifestation as the spirit enfolds.

Let me never lose the feeling of you within my soul
And help me to remember that you will make me whole.
Help me to listen deep within to that voice in my mind
That gives me guidance and wisdom of a spiritual kind.
Thank you for always being there and never leaving me.
Remind me if I drift too far that it is I and never Thee.

Oh, God, restore my faith and heal my broken spirit.
Let me know you in the special way that only I can feel it.

UNFAIR

If you think this government is fair
Look at the case of Leonard Peltiere.
Or Randy Weaver whose family is dead
By FBI bullets in their heads.
And what did Randy Weaver do?
Exactly what the government asked him to.

Or Raymond Wallace, who was shot in the head
When police broke in while he was in bed.
Or Waco, Texas where Branch Davidians were left
Totally dead by the ATF.

Or woman in prison because of a mate
Who did something to seal her fate
Whatever happened was something she knew
And that made her guilty, too.

The justice system is not fair
The citizens must learn to care.
Do something, change things before it's too late,
We do not have the time to sit and wait,
For if we do, it will seal our fate.

OUR OWN PRISON

All of us live in a prison
We make it for ourselves.
Some have bars and walls
And others are regular cells.

We build our prisons daily
By what we think we need
Which is more than the essentials
Often motivated by greed.

Our prison may be a house
With a mortgage way too high,
Or stocks and bonds and money
To build "security" to the sky.

Still other people's prison
Is a place they call "work."
They tie and bind themselves
To duties they mustn't shirk.

Still other people's prison
Is form and style and ritual
Which they think is religion
But of which is nothing spiritual.

Some people make a prison
Of helping others out.
Then they depend on you
And you are bound without a doubt.

Give me no prisons
In thought, word, or deed.
Let me live my life always
Because I know I am free.

THE AMERICAN WAY

I used to believe that freedom
Was the American way
Until without a trial
The judge sent me away.

The constitution states
No imprisonment without a trial.
Even on an appeal
There still was a denial.

What has happened to this country
That our forefathers founded?
The constitution was written
And extremely well grounded.

How did it happen that
Our rights were taken away?
Government grew too large
And the people had no say.

Most people don't know
And neither do they care.
They live inside their own little world
Not knowing what happens out there.

If "we the people"
Don't wake up soon
And fix this country
We'll all be doomed.

Somebody out there listen
Before it is too late.
The problems won't get better
And we have no time to wait.

MODUS OPERANDI

No crime, no trial, no sentence,
If I'm not a prisoner,
Why am I in prison?

Uniforms, guards, locks and cells,
If I'm not a prisoner,
Why am I in jail?

Shackles, handcuffs, chains, and keys.
If I'm not a prisoner,
Why do they use these?

Telephone tapes, people watching me,
If I'm not a prisoner,
What else could I be?

What gives them the right
To put me in prison
Then say I'm not a prisoner?

I have no choice except to stay.
I dare not run away.
I will not be a prisoner.

The only thing that I can be
Is live within my mind.
For it is always free.

They may lock up my body,
But they will never have me,
For the depth of my spirit is always free.

FREEDOM

Peace is not more important than
Freedom.

Freedom is dependent on
Responsibility.

We must accept
Responsibility.

We must cherish
Freedom.

Then we may learn to live in
Peace.

Justice collides with truth
like a storm with the sunlight
and evil with good.

There is no justice
Only people who act as
Kings of the jungle.

If justice is blind
Can truth be victorious?
Truthfully, not ever.

Can my words be like
the eternal mountains or
disappear like fog?

When thousands of words
come together in order
A story appears.

People are cleansed
like the earth purges herself
through wind, storms and fire.

God used my feet.
I didn't like where He sent me.
I went any way.

APPENDIX B

Resources for Prisoners

The Agape Church of Religious Science
1849 Centinela Ave.
Santa Monica, CA 90404
(310) 829-2780

FAMM (Families Against Mandatory Minimums)
c/o Mr. Robert Olson
P.O. Box 16241
St. Paul
MN 55116

Membership Unit
Fortune Society
29 W. 19th St.
New York, NY 10011
(214) 206-7070

Human Kindness Foundation
Rt. 1 Box 201-N
Durham, NC 27705
(919) 942-2138

Muriel Rukeper Poetry Wall
The Cathedral of St. John the Divine
1047 Amsterdam Ave.
New York, NY 10025

National Veterans Legal Services Project
Ronald Abrams
2001 S. St. NW Suite 610
Washington, DC 20009
(202) 686-2599
(202) 265-8305

P.E.N. American Center
Coordinator/ Prison Writing Project
568 Broadway
New York, NY 10012
(212) 334-1600

Prison Life Foundation
350 Fifth Ave., Suite 1905
New York, NY 10118

www.suite101.com
Prisoner Advocacy and Criminal Justice
This is a column written by Lynn R. Hartz, Ph.D. that includes links to many more resources.

Printed in the United States
29485LVS00002B/181

9 781592 863532